Economic Change in China, *c.* 1800–1950

This latest addition to the successful student series *New Studies in Economic and Social History* provides a concise introduction to the economic history of one of the major world powers. China is probably the only major economy for which it is still not certain whether modern economic growth at the aggregate level had taken hold by the middle of the twentieth century. This introductory analysis of the process of economic change in China from the end of the eighteenth century to the middle of the twentieth looks at the nature of the traditional economy, covers the pressure it came under from both internal and external sources during the nineteenth century and assesses the evolution of modern features in the twentieth. With maps, tables and bibliography to guide the student, this concise study will provide an invaluable introduction to crucial aspects of Chinese history.

PHILIP RICHARDSON is Senior Lecturer in Economic History at the University of Bristol. He has travelled widely in China and lectured at the Universities of Fudan (Shanghai) and Yunnan (Kunming).

New Studies in Economic and Social History

Edited for the Economic History Society by
Michael Sanderson
University of East Anglia, Norwich

This series, specially commissioned by the Economic History Society, provides a guide to the current interpretations of the key themes of economic and social history in which advances have recently been made or in which there has been significant debate.

In recent times economic and social history has been one of the most flourishing areas of historical study. This has mirrored the increasing relevance of the economic and social sciences both in a student's choice of career and in forming a society at large more aware of the importance of these issues in their everyday lives. Moreover specialist interests in business, agricultural and welfare history, for example, have themselves burgeoned and there has been an increased interest in the economic development of the wider world. Stimulating as these scholarly developments have been for the specialist, the rapid advance of the subject and the quantity of new publications make it difficult for the reader to gain an overview of particular topics, let alone the whole field.

New Studies in Economic and Social History is intended for students and their teachers. It is designed to introduce them to fresh topics and to enable them to keep abreast of recent writing and debates. All the books in the series are written by a recognized authority in the subject, and the arguments and issues are set out in a critical but unpartisan fashion. The aim of the series is to survey the current state of scholarship, rather than to provide a set of pre-packaged conclusions.

The series had been edited since its inception in 1968 by Professors M. W. Flinn, T. C. Smout and L. A. Clarkson, and is currently edited by Dr Michael Sanderson. From 1968 it was published by Macmillan as *Studies in Economic History*, and after 1974 as *Studies in Economic and Social History*. From 1995 *New Studies in Economic and Social History* is being published on behalf of the Economic History Society by Cambridge University Press. This new series includes some of the titles previously published by Macmillan as well as new titles, and reflects the ongoing development throughout the world of this rich seam of history.

For a full list of titles in print, please see the end of the book.

Economic Change in China, *c.* 1800–1950

Prepared for the Economic History Society by

Philip Richardson
University of Bristol

PUBLISHED BY THE PRESS SYNDICATE OF THE UNIVERSITY OF CAMBRIDGE
The Pitt Building, Trumpington Street, Cambridge CB2 1RP, United Kingdom

CAMBRIDGE UNIVERSITY PRESS
The Edinburgh Building, Cambridge, CB2 2RU, UK   http://www.cup.cam.ac.uk
40 West 20th Street, New York, NY 10011–4211, USA   http://www.cup.org
10 Stamford Road, Oakleigh, Melbourne 3166, Australia

First published 1999

Printed in the United Kingdom at the University Press, Cambridge

Typeset in 10/12½ pt Plantin   [CE]

A catalogue record for this book is available from the British Library

Library of Congress cataloguing in publication data
Richardson, Philip.
Economic change in China, c. 1800–1950 / prepared for the Economic History
Society by Philip Richardson.
    p.   cm. – (New studies in economic and social history)
Includes bibliographical references and index.
ISBN 0 521 58396 9. – ISBN 0 521 63571 3 (pbk)
1. China – Economic conditions.   2. China – Economic policy.
I. Economic History Society.   II. Title.   III. Series.
HC427.R45   1999
330.951 – dc21   99–12835   CIP

ISBN 0 521 58396 9 hardback
ISBN 0 521 63571 3 paperback

Contents

Maps

Acknowledgements

In moving falteringly to the production of this work I have become indebted to Leslie Clarkson for initiating the process, to Michael Sanderson for his immense editorial support and patience, to Bernard Alford for his advice on an early draft, and to an anonymous referee for suggesting an array of crucial improvements. I would also like to express my thanks to all of the Special Subject students with whom I had the pleasure of sharing so many Wednesday and Thursday mornings at various locations in Woodland Road and through whom I was able to test, refine and develop my ideas. Nor would the final product have been possible without the help of the map technicians in the Department of Geography at the University of Bristol. Despite them all the faults that remain are my own.

My thanks also to Gillian, Natasha and Emily, who have, at times, endured more in the way of my physical and emotional detachment that I had any right to impose and to Anne Griffiths not just for her fortitude in typing so many draft versions but for her tolerance towards my first fumbling and frustrating steps into the world of word-processing.

I am also grateful, beyond my capacity to express in words, to one particular family in Chengdu through whom I have come to feel closer to an understanding of the complexities, ambiguities and contradictions of China and its history than I had ever thought possible. And last, but by no means least, my thanks to China, simply for being there.

Note on references

References in the text within square brackets relate to the num-
bered items in the bibliography, giving the relevant page number
for each reference; for example [1:25–6; 15:42; 35].

Guide to pronunciation

This book uses the pinyin system. It is the official romanisation system adopted in the People's Republic of China and is employed by most international agencies. The former Wade–Giles usage is provided in the text for reference.

Pinyin	Wade–Giles
a	f*a*r
b	*b*e
c	i*ts*
ch	*ch*urch
d	*d*ay
e	h*e*r with silent 'r'
ei	w*ay*
f	*f*oot
g	*g*o
h	*h*ay
i	s*i*r with c, ch, r, s, sh, z, zh
i	*ea*t with other consonants
ie	*ye*s
j	*j*eep
k	*k*ind
l	*l*ay
m	*m*e
n	*n*o
o	s*aw*
ou	kn*ow*
p	*p*ay
q	*ch*eer
r	*r*um/leisu*r*e
s	*s*ister

sh	*sh*ort
t	*t*op
u (u)	r*u*de (German u)
w	*w*ant
x	*sh*e or *x*iesta
y	*y*et
z	*z*ero or rea*ds*
zh	ju*dg*e

Dynastic chronology

618–907   Tang (T'ang)
960–1279   Song (Sung)
1279–1368 Yuan
1368–1644 Ming
1644–1911 Qing (Ch'ing)
1912–49   Republic of China
1949–   People's Republic of China

Weights and measures

1 jin (chin) or (catty)	= 1.1 lbs.
2 jin	= 1 kilogram
100 jin	= 1 picul
1 picul	= 110 or 133 lbs.
1 shi (rice)	= 130 jin
1 mu	= 0.1647 acre (0.1518 pre 1911)
6 mu	= 1 acre
1,000 cash	= 1 tael
1 tael	= 1.5 yuan (1930s)
1 yuan (Ch$)	= US $0.26 (1933)
1 Haiguan (Haikwan) Customs tael	= US $1.27 (1890), US $0.67 (1914), US $0.41 (1933)
c.i.f.	customs, insurance and freight
f.o.b.	free on board

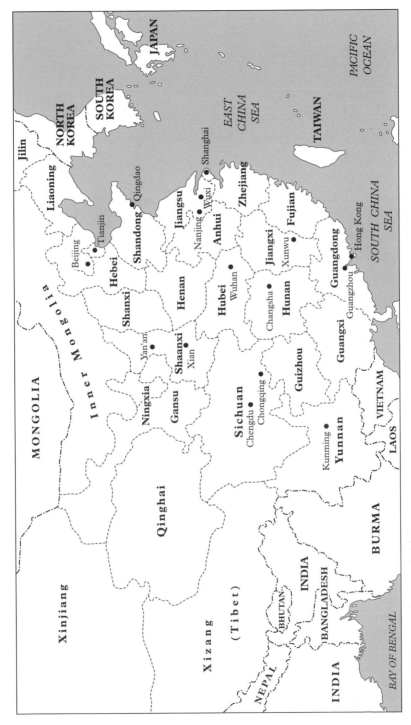

Map 1. China: provinces and cities.

Introduction

By the turn of the eighteenth century the economic expansion which had followed the Qing accession to power in the middle of the seventeenth century had begun to falter. In the early nineteenth century an impending crisis arising from a combination of internal problems which were novel in scale if not form was compounded by the effects of increasing Western intervention. Even if it was not realised at the time, it was no longer possible to progress or even contain the situation by employing exclusively traditional, Chinese, solutions. The subsequent interface between a pre-modern and still essentially traditional agrarian economy under pressure from within and the example (and the physical presence) of a modernising, industrialising West was mismanaged – by both sides. The Chinese body politic neither avoided nor embraced modernisation whilst for the West the lure of a vast Chinese market continued to outshine the reality. For a century across the late Qing and Republican periods the economy faced the conjunction of an inexorable population rise, continued Western penetration and internal political, social and military instability.

As a result, whilst in the middle of the eighteenth century China still stood as one of the most productive and technologically sophisticated economies in a pre-modern world, two centuries later it appeared as one of the more backward in a modern, industrialised era. It was, and remained, what Wrigley, in a different context, has termed an 'advanced organic economy' [16]. Indeed China, in many ways, represents *the* advanced organic economy *par excellence*. It continued to be predominantly traditional and overwhelmingly characterised by muscle-power.

Although increasingly influenced by the external forces of modernisation, the economy, on the eve of the Communist take-over in 1949, still awaited its technological transformation and was yet to make the transition to a mineral-based energy nexus or embrace urban industrialisation as its driving force.

The economy was not, however, entirely devoid of dynamism and it would be quite wrong to portray China as exclusively traditional and stagnant, failing to generate any elements of modern economic growth. Even if the economy did not 'modernise' fully in a Western sense, it did continue to experience change – with both Chinese and Western characteristics. It could not have accommodated such a prodigious population rise (from *c.* 30 million in 1800 to almost 600 million by 1950) or adjusted to increased contact with (and progressive integration into) the international economy without demonstrating a capacity for adaptability and the ability to produce and distribute different products in different ways.

The underlying issues in China's modern economic history can be posed in their simplest and most neutral form as how and why did the economy change in the way that it did to the extent that it did in the century and a half following the emergence of industrialism in the West? Almost inevitably from a Western perspective there has been a tendency to impose a negative comparative context on the search for answers. Why did Europe and not China produce an industrial revolution in the late eighteenth and early nineteenth centuries? And why, subsequently, did China fail to emulate an industrialising West?

One of the assumptions that underlies this Western-centric approach is that the Chinese experience can be explained in terms of the absence of the factors that are perceived to have determined the course of events in the West. But divergence from the European experience does not imply failure and it is important to recognise that China may have been different, not just superficially or in degree but in some of its fundamentals. The underlying philosophy was different, for example, and whereas Western societies operated, and were ruled through, a defined legal framework China rested on a moral code. That moral framework influenced the activities of the state and the ways in which markets functioned. The political economies differed, too, and it is inappropriate to attempt to designate the Chinese state as strong or weak in Western terms because it was not its purpose to be so. Similarly, the moral basis of the market and the various institutions that it spawned should caution against any automatic and unqualified application of the logic of the free market [8: 84; 15: 72].

A second problem stems from the periodisations that have been employed in the analysis of China's economic history. These have derived either from political divisions – between early (or High) and late Qing with a dividing line somewhere in the early nineteenth century – or from distinctions between traditional and modern economies/eras or between pre-modern, early modern and modern epochs. Myers, for example, employs the criteria of population growth, employment and income distribution to distinguish between pre-modern, early modern and modern development with the pivotal early modern interlude between 1895 and 1950 characterised by conditions of economic dualism and limited modernisation [11: 5–22]. Even if the temptation to equate modern with Western is resisted and all of the connotations of European early modern development set aside, it is also necessary to eschew any assumption that all traditional pre-modern elements were inimical to modernisation.

Definitions of 'pre-modern', 'traditional' and 'modern' economies are fraught with difficulty. In this enquiry the term 'pre-modern' as applied to China is taken to represent an economy continuing to operate on the basis of organic sources of power where economic relationships were the product of long-standing, distinctive, 'traditional' beliefs and practices. This should not, of course, necessarily imply an economy that was incapable of accommodating substantial population growth or of generating increases in per capita output and incomes. The term 'modern' signifies an economy in which sustained and sustainable increases in per capita incomes are evident and where a technological transformation of industry and agriculture has led to increased output and structural change.

The process of change towards that outcome is seen more as a continuum characterised by an interplay between traditional and emergent modern elements in which the former did not necessarily inhibit change or need to be abandoned in order for the latter to become dominant. Rather, the precise form of the course of change was conditioned and facilitated by traditional elements. In China change comprised elements which were direct Western incorporations, elements which were the product of Chinese adaptations of Western techniques, practices or ideas and elements which emerged entirely as indigenous responses to internal problems but which were, nonetheless, 'modern' in form.

The last twenty-five years have seen significant shifts in our understanding of the process of change in China. Indeed, there have been revolutions in both what is to be explained and how it is to be explained – even if the final outcomes of those revolutions are still uncertain. In brief, a consensus which once diagnosed failure to emulate the example of the Western economies and which emphasised continuing stagnation to the point of immiseration has been challenged by a new paradigm. This now stresses adaptability and dynamism and, at its most ambitious, postulates the onset of modern economic growth across the first half of the twentieth century, not just within the Treaty Port sector but also across the rural hinterland.

As a result, explanations which once took as their starting point (or which were directed towards) an unchanging economy, devoid of growth and lacking a technological revolution, now focus on the much more interesting search for a means of explaining how the Chinese economy might have succeeded in generating growth – and succeeded in the absence of a full technological transformation, despite recurrent political, social and military instability, and in the face of mounting population pressure and uninvited encroachment by foreign economic interests.

Without seeking to deny the influence of social, cultural and institutional factors the focus of the enquiry here lies with an exploration of economic variables. The concern is with the dynamics of the interplay between continuity and change which facilitated, inhibited and determined not just the process of change but the emergence of modern features within the Chinese economy and, perhaps, the development of a modern Chinese economy.

Four elements will occupy the centre stage. The first, the macro-economic growth record, covers the extent to which the economy changed. The others – the commercialisation of the land-scarce labour-abundant rural economy, the extent and nature of the relationship between the foreign sector and the domestic economy, and the economic role of the state – form the keys to an understanding of the process of change.

The experience of an economy in which one-quarter of the world's population continued to live, work and feed itself from less than 7 per cent of the world's cultivated acreage warrants consideration in its own right and as an end in itself. The analysis of that experience, however, also has a significance for a number of much wider issues which lie beyond the scope of this particular study. It has an obvious and immediate bearing on our understanding of one of the major political watersheds of the twentieth century – China's 'Liberation' from the forces of imperialism and feudalism in 1949. Was the peasant-based revolution that brought the communists to power the product of a feudal, stagnating economy being forced towards immiseration or did it grow out of a highly commercialised rural economy continuing to display a strong underlying dynamism and, perhaps, already exhibiting a capacity for growth and development? Secondly, did the subsequent transition to socialism build on rather than inaugurate modern economic growth and industrialisation? And, in the longer term, did the collective approach adopted in the 1950s subvert and destroy the dynamics of a successful market economy – dynamics which were to reappear, or were to be recreated, in the post-Mao reforms led by Deng Xiaoping?

In addition there is a wider international and comparative dimension. The analysis can illuminate our understanding of the adaptability of peasant societies and of the relationships between advanced and backward economies, between rural proto-industrialisation and urban industrial capitalism, and between capitalism, imperialism and modernisation. More than this, the analysis may challenge not only the universal applicability of Western-derived conceptualisations of modern economic growth but the validity of some of the assumptions upon which those conceptualisations rest.

1
Analytical frameworks

The analysis of the emergence of modern economic development in China has centred on four issues: the categorisation of the overall experience within the spectrum from decline through stagnation to growth and development; the extent of the foreign involvement and the nature of its relationship to the domestic economy; the complex interaction of forces which determined the dynamics of change in the increasingly labour-abundant land-scarce rural economy; and the role of the state.

The debate has progressed through a symbiotic interplay between the formulation of a series of theoretical constructs and the presentation of a widening body of empirical data. As methodological weaknesses in the constructs have been revealed, as the empirical perspective has changed and as the ideological and political parameters have fluctuated, new approaches have opened up, new priorities have emerged and the enquiry has moved on.

Analytical development, however, has not altogether brought resolution. There is still no firm consensus on how the overall historical growth trajectory should be characterised, on the significance of the foreign influence, or on the explanations for change in the rural sector. Moreover, there are doubts about whether the various individual conceptual frameworks can adequately explain the main features of China's economic history as they are perceived and, perhaps most seriously, there are question marks over the validity of some of the assumptions which underwrite those frameworks. For one leading writer in the late 1980s, the existing constructs had not provided, and could not provide, a persuasive explanation. The whole field was portrayed as having reached 'a paradigmatic crisis' where it was necessary to 'rethink assumptions and address the fundamental issues in new ways' [9: 299].

For at least two decades after 1949 most economic historians employed one of two very different approaches in their analysis of Chinese history, concentrating on either the effects of feudalism and imperialism or the relationship between tradition and modernity [33]. Chinese scholars preferred the former, Western scholars the latter. Chinese writers, inevitably, built their analysis around a Marxist framework. The economy was seen as pre-capitalist and feudal – or rather as 'semi-feudal' – to signify a partly colonial society undergoing the transition from feudalism to capitalism. The analysis centred on the extraction of surplus value from peasant producers by an exploitative ruling landlord class and on the fate of a 'natural' subsistence economy where farming and handicraft production were tightly integrated. In this picture Western imperialism served both to reinforce the feudal institutions (and thereby heighten the potential for exploitation) and to undermine the handicraft basis of the 'natural' economy.

The identification of 'incipient capitalism' in the form of certain elements of commercialisation and capitalist production offered a corrective variant to this diagnosis with its implied acceptance of a Western 'invention' of capitalism. But, even if no longer viewed as unchanging, the economy continued to be seen as backward and unable to advance into industrial capitalism not simply because the imperialist presence perpetuated feudal exploitation and destroyed the handicraft sector but also because Western capitalist enterprises pre-empted or 'oppressed' the indigenous 'capitalist sprouts' and drained resources from the economy [9].

Within the alternative paradigm the West was initially seen as representing, and offering to China, the superior and beneficial forces of modernisation. That China did not respond to this Western impact was accounted for in a Weberian manner by emphasising the inhibiting traditional conservatism of the Chinese culture and of its social, political and economic institutions [5]. Prevailing cultural values prevented the state from promoting, and the economy from taking advantage of, the forces of modernisation offered by the West. Change within tradition was the most that could be achieved [2: 57–78; 26: 9–10, 300]. Modernised enclaves were established in the Treaty Ports but the vast rural hinterland remained unaffected.

Some historians, perhaps instinctively, were cautious about accepting this exclusively, or even predominantly, socio-cultural interpretation and it began to be countered and revealed as unconvincing. The mutually exclusive dichotomy between tradition and modernity was challenged and there has been a growing recognition that, at the very least, the values and beliefs of the traditional society were not all incompatible with change or even development in a Western sense [2: 80–2]. Indeed, further research began to suggest that 'late-traditional Chinese values and ideas were in most respects already suitable for modern economic growth' [106: 380].

From an economic perspective two variants emerged. On one side there were those who resisted any idea of a self-evidently positive gift of Western modernisation and came to see imperialism as damaging to its host – a line which culminated in the application of the 'development of underdevelopment' thesis and veered more towards the Chinese viewpoint [24]. On the other came a more aggressive defence of the positive features of Western contact. Western intervention, it was argued, did not lead to the destruction of Chinese handicrafts or to the systematic 'oppression' of indigenous producers or to a net drain of resources from the economy. Rather the outcome was positive, if limited modernisation. For Hou, whatever development there was emanated from contact with the West [120] and more recently Rawski has re-emphasised the stimulus given to the Chinese economy by foreign trade and investment [92]. Paradoxically, a similar line was taken in the 1980s by some Chinese writers reflecting the changed perceptions of the Deng Xiaoping reform era [118].

In a sense Western and Chinese approaches were similar, for both assigned the dominant role in the shaping of China's modern economic history to the influence of the West. They also shared a common belief in the emergence of a dual economic structure with an advancing Western-inspired (or dominated) urban Treaty Port economy set against an unchanging and probably deteriorating traditional pre-modern rural economy. Both fostered a stagnationist view of the economy.

More recently, these approaches have come to be seen as

excessively Western-centric and empirically unsound. As Cohen has pointed out they rest on the application of paradigms derived largely from the Western European experience which cast the West in the role of catalyst to an otherwise static Chinese economic environment and assigned to the West the decisive influence on Chinese policy-making [2: 6]. The identification of this conceptual shortcoming was reinforced by the findings of a number of important empirical studies. There was, for example, a growing recognition that China's pre-modern economy already functioned as a sophisticated and integrated market system. In addition, it began to be argued that quantitatively the economic impact of the West was not as great, and could not have been as great, as had been thought or implied. The physical presence of the West was geographically modest (at least until the 1930s), the volume and value of flows of goods and financial services through the Treaty Ports were found to be small in relation to the economy as a whole and the composition of those flows was such that they were seldom competitive with indigenous suppliers [91; 108]. The Western impact, in short, could not have influenced the overall economic performance significantly one way or the other. It seemed that the major Western influence on China was on its psyche rather than in its pocket and that China's responses remained overwhelmingly directed towards solving problems in Chinese ways [53: 33, 92–107; 117: 30, 39]. As a result, neither the feudalism/imperialism nor the tradition/modernity dyads in their original formulations appeared capable of providing a satis-factory analysis of the process of change, particularly as far as the rural economy was concerned. New, and rather different, con-structs were required.

The way forward proved to be the application of a broadly Smithian classical approach which sought to encapsulate the Chinese experience within a framework which assigned the crucial dynamic role to the market against a background of population pressure on resources. The seminal work in what was to be a sequence of initiatives focusing on internal economic mechanisms was provided by Mark Elvin [4: 298–316].

Elvin's concern was to explain China's longer-term inability to maintain an earlier (twelfth-century) technological leadership and he sought to do so through what he defined as a 'high-level equilibrium trap' model. This Malthusian extrapolation postulates an economy in which technology (in this case pre-modern technology) determines the upper limit on the output generated by the available inputs of land and labour. Over time, as the technological frontier is reached, as best practice technology is generalised and as population presses on land the rate of output growth slows and eventually, with the onset of diminishing returns, becomes negative. An equilibrium position occurs when the potential output boundary is reached and intersects with the subsistence requirements of the population. Progress depends on raising the technological frontier and this can only be achieved by a breakthrough into modern technology. As the trap approaches closure, however, the surplus available for investment in that technology and the consumer demand base necessary to stimulate the breakthrough are both squeezed. The economy has neither the ability nor the incentive to advance.

In Elvin's view, this was precisely what was happening in China. Agricultural and industrial technologies were approaching, or had reached, their pre-modern frontiers. Crop yields were high even by modern standards and the existence of extensive commercial and transportation networks precluded a productivity boost from market integration. With the population rising more rapidly than land under cultivation, only a breakthrough into large-scale (and therefore expensive) modern technology could have held out the prospect of raising productivity levels significantly and so the creation of an income margin above subsistence. In these circumstances, the dominant agrarian economy could not finance, or stimulate the demand for, the industrial revolution in the non-agricultural sector necessary to facilitate the required breakthrough. China was caught in a high-level equilibrium trap. For Elvin, the impasse had been reached by the end of the eighteenth century. Others pushed the blockage forward. Dernberger argues for a closure by the end of the nineteenth century whilst Perkins selects the middle of the twentieth when the Manchurian safety valve had been exhausted [117: 26; 82: 32–5].

This approach proved highly influential, indeed some writers accepted the trap as the Chinese reality rather than as a device for analysing that reality. There are, however, a number of weaknesses with the model and its application, particularly for the period after

1800. In the first place it underestimates the capacity for low-level but cumulatively significant adjustment within a peasant economy. To postulate, even as a theoretical possibility, an economy which could operate at the full potential permitted by any technological frontier where all producers had adopted best-practice techniques would be to propose something remarkable – indeed unobtainable – about that economy. Secondly, even if the model is more persuasive in its analysis of the consequences of a convergence towards a trap closure its application has been undermined by calculations which suggest that there was still a substantial surplus over and above subsistence in the 1930s [93]. Furthermore, it is self-evident that after 1800, as modern technology and foreign capital became available, the trap could be raised.

Elvin, in fact, has abandoned the equilibrium trap as a means of analysing the post-eighteenth-century economy and now argues that the combination of low labour costs and the absorption of low-level modern technology served to reinforce the competitiveness of the pre-modern economic system and strengthen its hold. The problem was no longer one of 'paying for progress' but of 'making progress pay' and the result was a state of 'pre-modern over-development' in the hinterland [4].

A similar, although in important respects different, line of analysis was advanced by Kang Chao. Here the crucial theoretical intersect is not where total output equals subsistence requirements but the point at which the marginal product of labour in agricultural production equals its subsistence cost. Beyond this point, additional labour inputs cannot cover their subsistence requirements and a 'surplus' population arises. According to Chao China could, and did, not only reach this point but move much further beyond it than the European economies because population growth was determined more by cultural and social than by economic factors and because of the greater sophistication of the mechanisms for income distribution, both state and familial [1: 8–9]. This surplus labour force and the sub-subsistence wage that it commanded was the means by which household handicraft production could continue to compete with factory production and preserve the 'natural' economy. Non-transformative but limited advance was now seen as a function of the peculiarities of China's labour-surplus land-scarce economy.

Running parallel to these studies other, more quantitative, enquiries further undermined the picture of stagnation and some indicated the onset of growth and development in the twentieth century. There are virtually no quantitative data for the nineteenth century and even for the twentieth century the coverage is insufficient to allow a definitive picture to emerge. Nevertheless, John Chang's time series has established a growth rate in excess of 5 per cent for modern industrial production over the period 1912 to 1949 (9.4 per cent 1912 to 1936) [96: 71] and Perkins' early estimates identified a rise in national income and cautiously ruled out any fall in average per capita incomes [91: 122–3]. More recently Rawski has argued forcefully that the agricultural sector as well as the modern economy was characterised by output gains and, more significantly, advances in per capita incomes [92]. If confirmed, this will be crucial. In an agrarian economy welfare gains for the majority of the population were only possible if agricultural output (and incomes) rose more rapidly than population.

Explanations for these more optimistic findings were sought, in an extension of the modernisation thesis, through the logic of the market [12; 67; 79; 92]. The openness of the market structures which characterised the traditional economy, with large numbers of suppliers facing large numbers of consumers, indicates highly competitive product and factor markets. The more firmly this could be established, the more persuasively it could be argued that the rural economy approximated to perfectly competitive market conditions where producers took rational profit-maximising decisions and adjusted output and production techniques in response to changes in marginal costs and revenues. Rising output and increased labour productivity became the inevitable outcome of open, competitive and widening market conditions as China became more fully integrated into world markets from the late nineteenth century. The stagnation thesis had been turned on its head. Commercialisation, far from being the means by which the 'natural' economy and incipient capitalism were undermined, became the means by which growth was generated.

This new position, however, has not gained universal acceptance. There are reservations about Rawski's growth calculations and doubts have been expressed about the reality and the logic of perfectly competitive market commercialisation. For Huang, markets continued to be weighted against peasant producers and, whilst the rural economy was characterised by growth, it was growth without development [75; 76]. Output and family incomes may have risen, but labour productivity expressed in terms of output per unit of labour did not. Peasant producers were driven by a subsistence imperative rather than by the pursuit of profit maximisation. Peasant families 'involuted': they sought to protect incomes as they came under pressure from decreasing farm size by increasing labour inputs beyond the point where marginal revenue fell below subsistence needs.

In Huang's view, not only did the rural market structure fall far short of the perfectly competitive ideal, but peasants behaved irrationally in a classical Smithian sense. It was the paradox between vibrant commercialisation and falling labour productivity which, for Huang, lay at the heart of the paradigmatic crisis. Growth without development (defined as rising labour productivity) calls into question the universality of the classical (and indeed the Marxist) assumption that market-driven commercialisation inevitably induces a sequence of specialisation of function, efficiency gain, innovation, capital accumulation and development.

Most recently, R. Bin Wong has extended and deepened the application of Smithian dynamics by placing the analysis more firmly in a comparative Eurasian framework. Wong stresses the similarities between the European and Chinese experience prior to the nineteenth century in terms of population growth, agrarian development and proto-industrialisation, and reinforces the view that the subsequent transformation into rapid urban industrialisation represents a qualitative leap which was not inevitable and which was not predicted by contemporaries, even Adam Smith himself. For Wong, the dynamics of proto-industrialisation are analytically different from those of urban industrialisation and whereas Europe escaped from the limitations of the former China did not. What separated the two was the lack of agrarian class differentiation in China and Europe's historically specific ability to capture additional resources through overseas discoveries, to harness mineral sources of energy in an unprecedented manner and to enhance the momentum created by technical change through institutional innovation. This line of analysis only reinforces the danger of applying Eurocentric assumptions about the process of economic change and places stress on the viability and durability of the Smithian path of commercial expansion and specialisation and its relationship with the largely independent emergence of industrial capitalism which, in the case of China, did not take place until the first third of the twentieth century [15: 38–52].

Underpinning all of these approaches lies the need to recognise and accommodate China's physical heterogeneity. A variety of strategies has been suggested. There is the straightforward littoral (coastal)–hinterland (interior) dichotomy. There is Cohen's almost metaphysical distinction between the outermost, intermediate and innermost zones [2: 53–5], and Elvin's division between the Treaty Ports, the rural hinterland, the areas of adequate national resources (Manchuria and Taiwan) and Outer China (Inner Mongolia, Xinjiang and Tibet) [6]. And, within the agricultural economy, recognition needs to be made of both the major climatically determined crop variations and the high degree of local ecological variation [68; 74; 75]. Perhaps most influential is Skinner's 'macro-region' approach [30]. Here China (excluding Manchuria and Outer China) is divided into eight macro-regions most of which are the size of France (see map 2). The divisions are essentially topographical, in that each region possesses a geographical and technological distinctiveness encompassing within it a riverine core and a relatively less advanced periphery. These disaggregations can accommodate both spatial and temporal variation in the form and pace of change, but China's size and diversity determine that the experience of any one area, however defined, may well have little relevance for any other or for the economy as a whole.

The conclusion which follows from this historiographical survey of the various analytical approaches to China's economic history is that whilst none can provide all of the answers to the exclusion of the others, all are capable of providing insight into the complex and varied experience of the process of economic change. Indeed, all may be required if that complexity is to be encompassed. It should also be recognised that whilst there is no alternative but to generalise, almost all general characterisations of the Chinese experience are liable to be misleading.

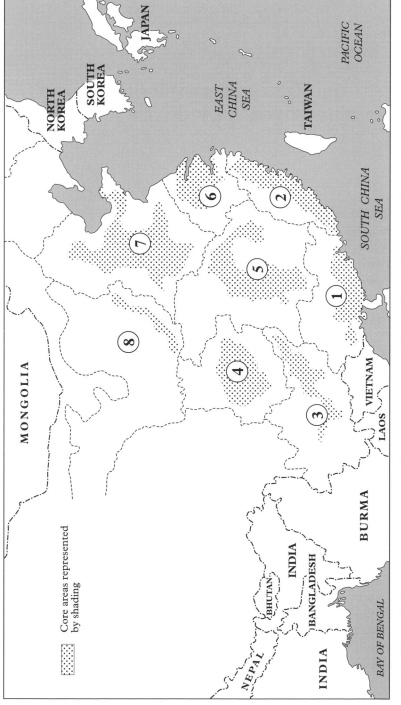

Map 2. China: physiographic macro-regions. Core areas represented by shading: 1. Lingnan; 2. Yun-gui; 3. Southeast coast; 4. Upper Yangzi; 5. Middle Yangzi; 6. Lower Yangzi; 7. North China; 8. Northwest China. Source: adapted from [3: 121–2; 30: 214–15].

2

The eighteenth-century legacy and the early nineteenth-century crisis

It is now clear beyond any doubt that the eighteenth century was a period of considerable secular expansion for an already commercialised, or rather 'commoditised', economy. A private, differentiated, market economy in which commodity flows in both absolute and per capita terms may initially have been higher than for any European economy, and in which rural industry may have been more widespread, experienced a long-term upswing in which output and population rose together without any apparent decline in per capita incomes. The economic expansion was also paralleled by the maintenance of the social stability which was the overriding aim of the ruling Confucian political economy [1: 25; 15: 42; 35: 256].

It is also clear that the market expansion, however vigorous, showed few signs of generating commercial, and none of industrial, capitalism. Extensive proto-industrialisation did not lead on to the development of any of the characteristics of modern factory-based industry. And the institutions which might have been able to promote (or take advantage of) any such changes were not forthcoming [15: 145–9]. China remained locked firmly in its Smithian, agrarian, dynamics and edged closer to its Malthusian boundaries. By the end of the century economic expansion and social stability were becoming more difficult to sustain. China had begun to fall behind Europe economically and, in retrospect, she was ill prepared to meet the economic, political and military challenges of the future.

The underlying momentum behind the expansion of both agricultural and industrial output was given by an expansion of population – it was to double to reach around 300 million during

the century – and its westward movement, though the government's promotional activities pursued within the context of the
traditional political economy of China's agrarian empire made an
important contribution. The destruction and depopulation in the
late Ming (early seventeenth century) had, temporarily, created a
relatively labour-scarce, land-surplus situation in the agricultural
sector. Even by 1700, when population probably still did not
exceed 150 million, the earlier losses had not been made good. As
they were, and as pressure on the land in the more densely
peopled eastern crescent grew, it was necessary to extend the area
of cultivation and increase productivity on existing farms. The
availability of the relatively tolerant but high-yielding New World
crops of maize and potatoes enabled migrants moving west to
clear, cultivate and survive on the wooded hill areas and other
marginal land. In the lowlands, the southern migration of wheat,
the extension of rice onto newly irrigated land and the spread of
early-cropping varieties enhanced the viability of farming [38:
100, 120]. The new strains permitted double-cropping – in many
areas not so much to achieve two crops of rice on the same land as
to permit a sequence of planting times on adjacent plots in order
to minimise the risk of crop losses due to adverse weather conditions. Although designed primarily to safeguard production,
higher output may well have been a consequence since the early-
ripening first harvest gave much more scope for planting a variety
of secondary (*zaliang*) crops [143: 114].

The government played an important role in initiating, sup-
porting and encouraging this expansion. Not only did it provide a
much greater measure of political and military security, it actively
promoted land clearance and the introduction of new crops and
crop rotations, offered tax incentives for immigrants, regularised
and eased the burden of the land-tax system by fixing it at a low
level, encouraged the commercialisation of the handicraft production system, became involved in restoring, improving and extending water control and irrigation facilities, and placed
considerable emphasis on establishing an effective granary system
[38: 23; 143: 134; 109: 77].

Despite the trend towards labour-intensive cash crops there was
still substantial seasonal underutilisation of labour and the rise in
population increased the need for the intensification of family

labour. This, together with an already established division of labour on gender grounds (men farm, women weave), provided the basis for the spread of rural industry and the development of many of the features of proto-industrialisation. The duplication of small producing units was encouraged by the government and facilitated by the growth of efficient and integrated merchanting networks [15: 143–4].

Most trade still took place within regional systems but there was a significant expansion of inter-regional and national trade in grain, cotton, silk and tea. By the beginning of the seventeenth century, commercialisation in the Yangzi Delta was already leading the way into specialisation of function in non-food crops – primarily silk and cotton. As a result, the growing population of the Delta drew in grain and other foodstuffs from coastal areas of China and South East Asia and from the interior, particularly the Middle Yangzi Basin. Internal provinces such as Hunan became, in effect, export areas, shipping rice almost a thousand miles down the Yangzi to Suzhou for distribution in the Delta. By the end of the eighteenth century Hunan, itself, was beginning to exhibit the same features of specialisation as the Delta. Upland farmers were growing and consuming sweet potatoes and placing their rice on the market for export. Lowland rice farmers were increasingly orientated to export production, and some were turning to tobacco and tea. The spread of commercialisation was gradual and took hold in different places at different times, but significant advances were made during the course of the century [35; 38]; so much so that in some areas local officials became concerned that over-commercialisation was undermining local grain self-sufficiency [109: 85].

Farmers, handicraft producers and merchants alike also benefited from gradually increasing prices as the money supply rose. China operated a bi-metallic currency. Copper was used for small local purchases and silver for long-distance settlement and the payment of taxes. In the eighteenth century output from the copper mines in Yunnan in the far southwest was considerably extended and supplies of domestic silver also rose. In addition, there was a massive inflow of silver as the result of China's balance-of-trade surplus with the outside world. After foreign trade was legalised in 1684 the expansion experienced in the late

Ming returned – there was a fivefold increase between the early 1720s and the 1760s and an eightfold increase by the end of the century. China exported increasing volumes of silk, tea and porcelain to other Asian economies and Europe but as yet there was little return market penetration. Silver flowed in, augmenting the money supply and leading to mild inflation [3: 127–9]. The trend towards increased monetisation was supported, particularly in the latter decades of the century, by the proliferation of 'native' and 'Shanxi' banks issuing their own paper currencies and providing more secure remittance facilities. By the early nineteenth century paper notes may have amounted to one-third or more of the total volume of money in circulation [38: 101].

The net effect of these developments was to raise the level of output as the population grew. But did the eighteenth century witness genuine modern economic growth in terms of sustained and sustainable increases in per capita output? The answer is that we simply do not know whether output per unit of land increased and, even if it did, whether output per person rose. It seems likely that the spread of new cropping techniques and irrigation improvement allowed productivity to rise in many areas of established cultivation. It is less certain whether productivity in the newly occupied peripheries reached the same level and any shortfall would have dragged the average down. Farming may have been highly productive in some of these areas (for example, Sichuan), but far less so in the hill country. However, the fact that the state was able to raise the capacity of the granaries significantly may be indicative of a surplus and the information that we have on population, agricultural prices and the money supply suggests productivity gains. In the Imperial province of Zhili (present day Hebei) population increased by 40 per cent between 1749 and 1790, whilst by the end of the century the prices of wheat, millet and sorghum rose by 34 per cent, 22 per cent and 33 per cent respectively from their 1738 to 1741 averages. At a national level Wang has calculated that whereas population rose on average by 0.72 per cent annually between 1700 and 1820 and the stock of silver rose by 0.9 per cent annually between 1680 and 1820, rice prices in the Delta rose on average by no more than 0.7 per cent per annum [173: 65]. It is likely that in a period of monetary inflation prices could only have been held at roughly the same rate as population growth if there had been some increase in productivity.

So, the eighteenth century as a whole was one of agricultural and proto-industrial expansion; of output rising in line with, and possibly ahead of, population. It was a period of increasing, perhaps unprecedented, commercialisation, of increasing diversity and complexity, of a shifting balance between public and private responsibility and control, of effective bureaucratic leadership and, probably, of increasing social mobility. Yet no mechanism to ensure sustained economic growth had been created. There is no evidence of the nature of production changing outside the agricultural sector. Technology did not change, there was no transition beyond the workshop towards the factory and the financial markets remained geared to enhancing circulation rather than promoting accumulation [7: 27; 95: 9–10]. Significant merchanting concentrations of wealth did not emerge and class divisions did not become evident. Smithian dynamics remained in place [15: 146].

For most, if not all, of the eighteenth century none of these developments seemed necessary and, within the confines of Confucian political economy, would have been regarded as potentially destabilising and undesirable. But by its turn signs of strain were beginning to show and by the 1830s the economy, like the dynastic system as a whole, was moving towards crisis. Moreover, it was precisely those same factors which lay behind the economic expansion that now contributed to the downturn in the cycle [38: 110].

By 1800 the population had probably exceeded 300 million. The Empire was larger than ever before and, with the incorporation of Xinjiang, Xizang (Tibet), Manchuria, Yunnan and Taiwan, was becoming increasingly difficult to manage. England at the time had a population of only 11 million, Russia only 40 million. By 1850, when China's population may have surpassed 400 million, it had reached a level which the United States has still to experience. Rates of growth, however, were beginning to slacken. An annual rate of increase of 0.7 or 0.8 per cent which prevailed over much of the eighteenth century fell to 0.4 or even 0.3 per cent by the middle of the nineteenth century, and the fall was probably a reflection of increasing economic pressure [38: 107;

173: 65]. Perdue sees this as an indication that the peripheral areas could no longer absorb large numbers of immigrants and that they were reaching the limits of their expansion [143: 59]. Ho has argued that the system could no longer sustain an increasing population without overstretching itself [169: 206] and in Chao's view grain yields had reached their peak [1: 215]. Contemporary officials had come to realise that population growth was not an unmixed blessing and in the 1790s 'China's Malthus', Hong Liangji, warned that population was increasing more rapidly than the means of subsistence [143: 61].

Agriculture was certainly much closer to, if it had not already reached, the limits of its capacity to adjust to further population increase, even in parts of Manchuria [38: 35; 169: 45–6]. The extractive nature of the frontier economy had imposed an ecological cost – denuded hillsides, soil erosion and increased silting had begun to reduce productivity locally and upset the delicate hydraulic balances downstream [38: 130–1]. In Hunan, there was a growing threat of ecological exhaustion in both lake and mountain areas [143: 236]. In the absence of additional fertilisers soil fertility was coming under pressure from increased double-cropping. Double-cropping could also have an adverse effect on the ability to keep livestock and, therefore, on the supply of manure. According to Wang, 1780 marked the transition from a half-century-long warm climate phase to a cooler cycle and the incidence of droughts and floods seems to have been much heavier in the period 1820 to 1850 [173: 62].

Moreover, the expansion of the economy and the maintenance of economic stability had become dependent on the continuation of an inflow of silver bullion [36: 7]. That inflow reached its peak in the first two decades of the new century but was then abruptly reversed as opium imports mounted in the mid 1820s. The estimates on the extent of the turnaround may vary, but its existence is undoubted. Between a quarter and a half of the silver inflow between 1700 and 1820 may have been lost in the next twenty years [38: 234–5; 173: 60–1]. According to Eastman, virtually the whole of the inflow from England was lost [3: 129].

Again, as had happened in the mid-seventeenth century, the effects on the economy were immediate and serious [36: 10–11]. The money supply contracted and prices dropped by as much as

40 per cent between 1820 and 1850, though on Wang's figures for the Delta the fall in the price of rice from the average of the early 1820s to that of the early 1850s was less than one-third, and much of that fall occurred after 1850 [173: 60–1, 78]. Nor was it just that the silver supply fell, reducing the amount of coinage and the backing available for the note issue, for the velocity of circulation also seems to have decreased as hoarding took place. In addition, an important change was taking place in the relative prices of silver and copper. Despite falling output from the copper mines in Yunnan, copper began to depreciate (by up to 50 per cent between 1820 and 1850). Farmers who received copper coin for their produce on the market but still had to pay their taxes in silver found themselves facing both falling prices and a depreciating copper exchange rate and, therefore, had to market more of their goods if they were to meet their tax obligations [3: 130].

The government, however, was no longer in a position to grant remissions. The various rebellions of the late eighteenth century had exhausted the accumulated budget surplus. Uprisings in Xinjiang and Sichuan cost a total of 100 million taels to suppress and the White Lotus Rebellion (1796 and 1806) another 100 million (although Wang gives the figure at 200 million) at a time when annual revenue did not exceed 100 million [38: 219; 173: 64–7]. The government had instituted a land-tax system which precluded increased revenue from agriculture by means other than an increase in registered land and the upsurge in commerce in the eighteenth century had remained un-taxed. The revenue base was no longer sufficient to cope with an unstable military situation and certainly in no state to provide tax remissions or to finance public works as a means of generating employment.

The target holdings for the 'ever normal' granaries, whose purpose was to balance between harvest fluctuations, reached their peak levels of 45 million shi (about 3 million tonnes) in the 1790s [152: 21]. In the Imperial province of Zhili (Hebei) stores of 3.5 million shi had fallen to 600,000 by 1833 [172: 76]. Although these figures indicate a decline in the granary system it should be noted that in Zhili there was still sufficient grain in storage to feed 3 million poor families of four for a week and this takes no account of the community and charity granaries. It is also necessary to recognise that there had been a shift in the balance between grain storage and dispersements of silver as the preferred method of intervention [152: 478–9].

The increased incidence of social unrest was, in part at least, the product of the economic expansion of the eighteenth century and was exacerbated by the decline in the quality of the bureaucracy and the increase in corruption by both officials and local gentry. The emigration into the frontier areas had not been matched by an expansion of bureaucratic control while the privatisation of commerce and administrative function gave the government less leverage in times of need. By the end of the century antagonisms between immigrants and the indigenous populations were growing. Ethnic and religious minority tensions were on the increase. In the eighteenth century much of this could be contained through litigation, but by the nineteenth century it was spilling over into uncontrolled violence. Piracy, smuggling and open banditry were on the increase and were all symptoms of a worsening economic climate and a loss of central control [38: 132–7].

By the end of the eighteenth century natural disasters, the defiance of Imperial edicts, and rising local conflicts in Hunan and Hubei provinces were all forerunners of the much larger-scale disorder to come. And in the 1830s there were grain blockages as localities sought to protect precarious supplies against the demands of export merchants and the military. Tax arrears were rising and in the 1840s there were tax-resistance riots. Economic problems created social discontent and it was this discontent which could be, and was, tapped into by the Taiping rebels as they passed through in a movement that was to engulf much of south and central China and was seriously to undermine the economy in the 1850s [143: 238–51].

The momentum had been lost and many of the forces propelling the economy forward in the eighteenth century were to restrain it in the nineteenth. The political authority of the centre had been undermined and population pressure, together with the commercialisation of the administration and the further privatisation of trade, had created tensions – particularly in the newly created periphery – which threatened the structure as a whole. Growth, or rather economic expansion and prosperity, may have come to be taken for granted and the downward adjustment was a painful one. Consumerism, which in China pre-dated capitalism, had continued to develop, but without producing capitalism; and it had left China vulnerable to the threat of capitalism from outside in the new century. Could population growth and subsistence family incomes be sustained in the long term through exclusively Smithian dynamics in which an increasing reliance was placed on cash cropping and the integration of handicraft pursuits within the rural economy?

Initially, the problems were diagnosed as internal and familiar. As such it was thought that they could be contained within the tradition. But whilst the symptoms may have been seen before, the dimension of the problem was novel. The situation had changed. Chinese solutions to traditional Chinese problems by traditional Chinese means could no longer be pursued in isolation. The West, an industrialising capitalist West, was beginning to impinge. It was adding to, and changing the nature of, the problem. Ultimately, new responses were needed, not just to allow expansion to continue but to ensure that the system could survive. Change was necessary if output was to continue to keep pace with population and maintain the livelihood of the people, and if the gap between China and the West was not to widen even more rapidly.

3
Growth and structural change

The attempt to quantify *ex post facto* the level, structure and growth of national income prior to 1949 offers the means by which the timing of the onset of modern economic growth (defined as sustained increases in aggregate and per capita output) can be established and the emergence of structural change associated with modernisation identified. The construction of estimates for the individual components of a nation's income (Gross Domestic Product (GDP) is the conventional measure in the literature on China) is a difficult and complex process. It requires an intimate understanding of the nature of the Chinese economy, a familiarity with the available data and an acute awareness of their limitations, and a command over the statistical techniques involved in national income accounting.

Any discussion of the outcome of the various attempts to quantify China's economic experience must, out of caution, begin with a health warning concerning their ability to reflect accurately the contemporary economic reality. There was no systematic compilation of statistics, either governmental or private, for output or income prior to the 1950s. As a result, the cupboard labelled 'quantitative data' is bare for the nineteenth century and less than half-stocked for the first half of the twentieth. No more than the first tentative steps towards uncovering the structure and growth of national income have been taken and it is only for modern industry that it has been possible to compile a series which commands confidence [92: 85]. Of necessity the construction of estimates for the remaining components of national income rests on a process of induction and extrapolation. None can be regarded as definitive. All remain highly sensitive to the accuracy and representativeness of the evidence and to the validity of the assumptions built in to the calculations. As additional evidence has been mobilised and as the assumptions have acquired more elaborate theoretical justification, some of the areas of uncertainty have been reduced, although substantial margins of error persist and many of the component estimates remain plausible but unproven.

The analysis of the level and structure of national income within the Western literature has developed from three separate snapshot measurements of the economy – by Chang Chung-li for the 1880s, by Perkins for 1914/18 and by Liu and Yeh for 1933 [41; 91; 90]. Chang's figures have been revised (upwards) by Feuerwerker but still do no more than 'roughly indicate the relative sizes ... of the several sectors of the economy' [43: 2]. Perkins' extremely tentative estimates have been disaggregated and amended by Yeh [94]. The more comprehensive and detailed estimates for 1933 have gained a wider measure of acceptance though the agricultural component has been revised (downwards) by Perkins [82]. Yeh has accepted this revision and has extrapolated backwards and forwards to provide figures for the years 1931 to 1936 in order to obviate the reliance on a single depression year [94]. The analysis of long-term change across the first half of the twentieth century rests on the performance of the economy between the bench-mark years 1914/18 and 1931/6. The use of 1914/18 (a boom period) and 1931/6 (covering the international depression) as terminal years should avoid any cyclical overstatement and create the potential for significant error in a downward direction. Beyond 1936 the economy was disrupted by war.

The findings on the level and structure of GDP are set out in tables 1 and 2 and the growth-rate estimates are given in table 3. They reveal an economy dominated by pre-modern production in general and by agriculture in particular. As Feuerwerker puts it, in the 1880s there was little of the economy 'that was not included within the agricultural sector or quite intimately connected with it' [43: 1]. In the 1930s, agriculture still accounted for almost two-thirds of GDP, with modern industry (defined as manufacturing, mining, utilities and construction) contributing only 7.5 per cent [91]. A similar picture is revealed on the expenditure side, with personal consumption accounting for almost 90 per cent of national income [53]. Investment and government services at no

Table 1. *Sectoral contributions to gross domestic product 1880s–1936 (%)*

	1880s	1914/18	1931/6	1933
Agriculture	**67.1**	**66.0**	**62.9**	**65.0 (64.0)**
Industry	**7.1**	**16.1**	**18.9**	**17.2 (17.8)**
Mining, manufacturing, utilities	5.3	9.4	11.6	10.4
Construction	0.9	1.1	1.6	1.2
Transport	0.9	5.6	5.7	5.6
Services	**26.0**	**17.9**	**18.2**	**17.7 (18.2)**
Trade	6.6	9.2	9.3	9.4
Finance	2.2	0.7	1.0	0.7
Rent	4.9	3.7	3.6	3.6
Government services	4.9	3.1	3.1	2.8
Other services	7.2	1.2	1.2	1.2
Depreciation				1.0
	100	**100**	**100**	**100**
	Million taels	Billion 1933 yuan	Billion 1933 yuan	Billion 1933 yuan
GDP	3,327	24.26	29.13	29.88

Sources: 1880s [41: 296; 43: 2]; 1914/18 [94: 126]; 1931/6 [94: 126]; 1933 [90: 66; 91: 139].

Table 2. *Composition of gross domestic expenditure 1931/6 (%)*

	Yeh	Rawski
Personal consumption	92.3	83.3
Government consumption	5.1	11.0
Gross domestic investment	5.1	6.0
Net exports	−0.2	−0.3

Sources: [94: 98; 92: 341].

Table 3. *Growth of GDP 1914/18–1931/6 (% per annum)*

	Perkins	Yeh	Rawski
GDP	1.4	1.1	1.8–2.0
Population, Perkins variant	0.9	0.9	0.9
GDP per capita	0.5	0.2	1.1
Population, Schran variant	0.6	0.6	0.6
GDP per capita	0.8	0.5	1.2

It should be noted that the Perkins rate of growth is calculated using 1957 prices. The relative prices of agricultural and industrial prices were very different in the 1950s and this has the effect of reducing the share of agriculture in GDP and thus understating the rate of growth of total output. If the population for 1914/18 is taken to be 440 million rather than 430 million (to allow for growth since 1913) the Perkins variant GDP per capita figures need to be raised.
Source: [92: 330–1].

more than 5 per cent each remained essentially pre-modern in their contribution. And agriculture still provided employment for over 80 per cent of the labour force. Structural change was, however, clearly under way. The industrial sector as a whole increased its share from 16.1 per cent to 18.9 per cent between 1914/18 and 1931/6 and modern industry grew by about 9 per cent per annum to increase its share from 3.5 per cent to 7.5 per cent [92; 94].

The continuing lack of precision over the course of demographic change in the century prior to 1950 imposes an additional element of uncertainty into the calculation of per capita incomes and output. Two alternative population scenarios are available (table 4). Perkins' figures indicate a slow upward movement of population (0.5 per cent per annum) after the devastating effects of the

Table 4. *Population estimates 1850–1933 (million)*

	Perkins	Schran
1850	410 ± 25	430
1873	350 ± 25	420
1880	367	436
1893	385 ± 25	453
1913	430 ± 25	491
1914/18	440	500
1933 (1931/6)	500 ± 25	550

The figures for 1880 and 1914/18 are extrapolations from the 1873, 1893 and 1913 estimates.
Sources: [82: 16, 216; 171: 644].

Taiping Rebellion followed by a more rapid expansion after 1913 (0.8 per cent per annum) to reach 500 million in 1933 [82]. Schran, by contrast, argues that this figure of 500 million is not consistent with the known population level of 582 million (as recorded in the census of June 1953) in view of the massive demographic losses (20 to 30 million) sustained during the 'war and revolution' decade 1937 to 1949. Rather Schran argues for a more stable underlying rate of expansion of 0.6 per cent per annum with the population reaching 491 million in 1913 and 550 million in 1933 [171]. Acceptance of the higher population figures implies lower absolute levels of average per capita incomes but a higher rate of growth in those incomes over the period. The logic behind Schran's position seems impeccable, though his conclusions have not received widespread support and both estimates are employed in order to create alternative boundaries.

Neither Perkins nor Yeh see their estimates for aggregate output as demonstrating clear real per capita gains in the twentieth century (table 3). Growth is evident in total output but, given the degree of error inherent in the data, not by a sufficient margin over population to do any more than rule out the likelihood that the per capita position deteriorated. Unequivocal average income gains depend on the demonstration of rising per capita agricultural output and Yeh and Perkins do not claim this. In fact, their estimates indicate a falling per capita output of food grain. If anything, it is the period prior to 1914 which emerges as the more

Table 5. *Average GDP per capita grain (rice) purchasing capacity (calories/day)*

	1880s	1914/18	1931/6	1933
GDP (million taels or billion 1933 yuan)[a]	3.327	24.6	29.13	29.88
Population (million)[b]	367/436	440/500	500/550	500/550
GDP/per capita (taels or 1933 yuan)	9.07/7.63	55.9/49.2	58.3/53.0	59.8/54.3
Rice/picul (taels or 1933 yuan)[c]	1.28	3.50	3.50	3.50
Average per capita consumption (piculs)	7.09/5.96	16.0/14.1	16.6/15.1	17.1/15.5
Average daily calories[d]	3,438/2,890	7,759/6,838	8,050/7,322	8,292/7,516

[a] See table 1.
[b] See table 4.
[c] [41: 303; 82: 288; 90: 136, 325, 330].
[d] Calculated at 177,000 calories per picul [90: 29].

Table 6. *Average per capita grain availability (calories/day), 1880s–1936*

	Output (million piculs)	Population (million)	Average calories (A)[a]	Average calories (B)[b]
1880s (Chang/Feuerwerker)	1,715	367	1,214	1,535
		440	1,012	1,219
1914/18 (Perkins/Yeh)	2,833	440	1,755	2,114
		500	1,544	1,860
1931/6 (Yeh)	3,038	500	1,656	1,995
		550	1,505	1,813
1931/6 (Perkins)	3,200	500	1,744	2,101
		550	1,744	1,910
1933 (Liu and Yeh)	3,456	500	1,884	2,270
		550	1,713	2,063
1929/33 (Buck)	3,638	592	1,675	2,023

[a] Assumes a food coefficient of 0.76, an extraction coefficient of 0.77 and a calorie conversion rate of 177,000 per picul [90: 29].

[b] Assumes a food coefficient of 0.855, an extraction coefficient of 0.81 and a calorie conversion rate of 175,000 per picul [69: 68–9].

dynamic, since grain output increased by 73 per cent between the 1880s and 1914/18 against only 7 per cent between 1914/18 and 1931/6. Whilst this pre-1914 expansion is consistent with the rising price trend of the period and with intensified commercialisation as China began to be more fully integrated into the international economy from the 1890s, the rate of growth seems unduly high and suggests that the estimates for one or both of the terminal dates are inaccurate.

That the Feuerwerker figure for the 1880s is an underestimate is indicated by the extremely low level of average per capita income that it implies. The use of average money incomes can be meaningless but a base-line can be created by converting average per capita income to its current purchasing power in terms of the dominant food source (in this case rice) and, therefore, to daily calorific intake. Feuerwerker's figures indicate a society in which the expenditure of the whole of the average per capita GDP on rice would have given a calorie intake of only 2,890 to 3,438 calories per day (depending on which population estimate is chosen). Moreover, the estimate for total grain output suggests a level capable of providing an average daily intake of little more than 1,500 and perhaps as low as 1,000 calories (tables 5 and 6). Whilst these figures need to be supplemented by the non-grain calorie intake, the standard subsistence is normally taken to be about 2,000 calories daily. It should also be noted that the metabolism for such a highly vegetarian diet may be less efficient and that the estimates indicate availability rather than actual intake [69: 50].

But are the crucial control figures for 1933 (or 1931/6) and 1914/18 any more reliable? How persuasive are the growth trends which they indicate? And are Rawski's more recent estimates any more accurate and plausible? Liu and Yeh regarded 85 per cent of the components in their calculations for 1933 as 'hard', with 'hard' defined as categories where '*relatively* good data are available only for *certain parts* of that sector' (my italics) [90: 69–70]. The agricultural estimates are the most obvious weak point and, because of their crucial importance, warrant particular comment. In the absence of direct output evidence Liu and Yeh derived their estimates from figures for land under cultivation and crop yields. They selected a yield point roughly mid-way between the Buck and the National Agricultural Research Bureau survey results.

Table 7. *Sectoral annual growth rates 1914/18–1931/6*

	Weight	Yeh	Rawski (preferred)
Agriculture	0.629	0.8	1.4–1.7
Industry (modern)	0.042	7.7	8.1
Handicrafts	0.075	0.7	1.4
Construction			
Transport and communications:	0.016	3.5	4.6
Modern	0.017	4.0	3.0
Traditional	0.039	0.3	1.9
Trade	0.093	1.1	2.5
Finance	0.010	2.9	5.0
Government services	0.031	1.0	3.4
Personal services	0.012	0.8	1.5
Residential rent	0.036	0.9	1.5
Total	1.000	1.1	1.8–2.0

Source: [92: 330–1].

Perkins, however, pointed out that this compromise implies crop yields in the 1930s higher than those recorded for 1957 and revised the estimate down by 9 per cent. This is an adjustment which, despite citing evidence to the contrary, Yeh has subsequently accepted. In fact, Myers has subsequently presented data which do indicate that yields were higher in the 1930s [80] and an acceptance of the revised Perkins/Yeh position implies a grain output which, even allowing for imports, would have permitted daily per capita grain consumption levels of no more than 1,800 calories (table 6). It is possible, therefore, that the revised estimates understate the level of agricultural output.

The estimates for 1914/18 are far more tenuous. The Perkins agricultural output figure is based on the assumption that yields equalled those of 1957 whilst handicraft output is taken to be identical to that of 1933 and services are arbitrarily assigned a 25 per cent increase over the period [91]. Yeh assumes that handicraft output moved more closely in line with population and adopts a more modest expansion for the service sector (see table 3) [94]. Neither consider the reliability of their estimates to be sufficient to demonstrate growth in per capita terms across the period, though that is what they indicate.

Rawski is less concerned with identifying the level of GDP at any point in time than with establishing the rate of growth across the period. Recognising the inherent difficulties in calculating output levels for 1914/18, Rawski has extended the coverage of Chang's output series for modern industry and constructed proxy indicators for rates of change in the other components. Yeh's 1931/6 weights are then applied to the results in order to arrive at a growth rate for the economy as a whole (table 7). The resulting 'preferred' annual growth rate is 1.9 per cent, with agricultural output growing within the range 1.4 to 1.7 per cent. These figures in turn imply average real income gains in excess of 1 per cent. Rawski also claims that the share of national income devoted to investment rose from 7 to 11 per cent and the government sector increased its share of output to 6 per cent [92]. Rawski's position, therefore, is significantly more expansionary than those proffered by Yeh or Perkins and, if correct, would seem to point incontrovertibly both to sustained increases in average incomes and to the onset of modern economic growth. Indeed, Rawski interprets his findings as indicating that the Chinese economy was making progress at a rate which matched the comparative Japanese experience between 1897 and 1931 and marks a 'decisive upward break from historical patterns of economic evolution' [92: 336–7].

This interpretation has not gained universal endorsement. Indeed, the reaction in some quarters has been highly critical and it has been claimed that the unreliability of the data, the nature of the assertions built into the analysis and the lack of independent confirmation render the findings misleading, if not false. The robustness of Rawski's findings depends on the validity of the proposed proxy relationships and the accuracy and representativeness of the evidence used to calculate the behaviour of the proxies themselves. The growth estimates for the non-agricultural sectors (excluding manufacturing) rest on the following assumptions: that the growth of electricity supply can serve as a proxy for the rate of growth of output in the utilities sector as a whole, that value-added growth in cotton-textile handicrafts (1901/10–1931/6) can serve for that of all handicrafts (1914/18–1931/6) and that the increases in the volume of freight traffic can accurately indicate the rate of growth of value added in transportation and (in a slightly different form) trade. Rawsti also assumes that the rate of growth of gross domestic fixed capital formation mirrors that of construction, that the rate of growth of the money supply forms a proxy for output growth in finance, that the value added by residential rents and personal services moved with population, and that the rate of growth of long-term rural wage rates equalled that of agricultural productivity and real incomes [92].

In principle these assumptions are sufficiently acceptable to carry the analysis forward, though considerable caution does need to be exercised regarding Rawski's manipulation of the data in arriving at the precise estimates. A few examples serve as illustration. In the case of construction, the growth rate for the proxies (4.6 per cent) rests on accepting Rawski's own 'suggestion' that the ratio of Gross Domestic Fixed Capital Formation (GDFCF) to GDP rose from 7 to 11 per cent (a ratio which itself suffers from the 'inhibiting effect of extreme uncertainty') and the acceptance of the 'preferred' rate of growth for total output (the result that Rawski is endeavouring to reveal) [92: 260]. The investment calculations, moreover, themselves rest on two further sets of assumptions. Rawski follows the precedent set by Svennilson for the European economy in the inter-war years by arguing that capital formation in the modern sector can be calculated as the geometric mean of the quantity indices for cement and steel (though with machinery added). There is, however, no discussion of whether this approach can be transposed from Europe to an economy at a very different stage of development with fundamentally different resource endowments. Moreover, the largest single component in GDFCF (47 per cent) is accounted for by an allowance for agricultural depreciation and here Rawski adopts a rate of 7 per cent on the grounds that the corresponding estimates for Japan between 1895 and 1935 lie in the range 9.5–11.7 per cent [92: 253–5]. These shortcomings seriously undermine the reliability of the construction estimate and cast doubt on Rawski's ambitious claim for a rise in the investment ratio.

Similarly, in the case of transportation, Rawski offers rates of growth for the volume of freight traffic of 3 per cent (modern) and 1.9 per cent (traditional) to stand as proxies for value-added. The latter figure, however, is based on the assertions that seaborne junk traffic grew by 2 per cent per annum and land traffic (human and animal) by 1 per cent [92: 276]. The first of these suggestions is supported only by evidence that the value of junk-borne trade into five North China ports grew at 4.5 per cent annually in nominal terms and 1.4 per cent in real terms and that shipping tonnage in 'several (overlapping) major ports' rose at a rate of between 2.4 and 6.9 per cent [92: 205]. Finally, in producing estimates for rents and personal services, Rawski begins by accepting Yeh's assumption that they moved in line with population but in his 'preferred' version adopts figures which exceed the highest population estimate.

These criticisms notwithstanding, Rawski's findings for the non-agricultural sectors, though still far from perfect, probably represent improvements on previous estimates. In the case of agriculture the doubts are much more serious. In brief, Rawski argues that the growth of total output can be given by the summation of the rates of growth of population and average per capita output. Alternative estimates for population change are available and Rawski proposes that the agricultural productivity gains can be inferred directly from the measurement of real incomes in the countryside. Two crucial assumptions underwrite this procedure: that per capita farm output moved in line with real incomes, and that the real incomes of self-employed farmers moved in tandem with the real wages of farm labourers [92: 323–9]. In short, the behaviour of real wages is taken as the proxy for the movement of per capita incomes and output. Although Rawski sets the relationships up as 'indicative', in the final analysis the rising trend of real wages for long-term farm labourers is taken as identical to that of real incomes and productivity across the sector as a whole.

The critique of this position has centred on two issues: is the view of the economy on which the assumptions rest a valid one and, even if it is, is the evidence strong enough to support the precise productivity gains suggested? Rawski's line of argument is founded on the assertion that the agricultural economy was highly commercialised, integrated and competitive to the point where it approximated to perfect market conditions. On this basis, Rawski is able to assume a neo-classical economy in which wage rates moved into equilibrium within, if not across, sectors and labour moved easily across rural–urban boundaries to achieve optimal returns. But if the market was less than perfect (and there is a substantial body of opinion that it was far from perfect) the correlation between wage rates and productivity becomes much more tenuous [162].

Turning to real wage rates themselves, Rawski relies heavily on Buck's money-wage data for one hundred counties deflated by price data for Wuchin county in Jiangsu. The data show average rises of 0.5 per cent for 1901 to 1933, 1.2 per cent for 1915 to 1933 and 2.1 per cent for 1925 to 1933, with median rates in the range 0.4 to 1.6 per cent. Rawski selects 0.8 as the central, 'preferred' rate though notes that the figures cannot be definitive because of the unsystematic nature of the Buck survey methods. It should be remembered that there was a predisposition in the Buck survey towards the more commercialised areas and towards larger farms, with information being gathered by students asking local informants to provide from memory material on farm wage rates going back over twenty years. It is not at all clear that these 'memory lane' data alone can substantiate precise findings on national trends and it is far from certain that it is acceptable to use price data from one county to extrapolate for the economy as a whole. There were significant regional (and even local) price variations and Wiens has pointed out that using alternative, disaggregated, price deflators real wages actually fell by 0.5 per cent in the north and rose by only 0.1 per cent in the south [166].

But these, and other, methodological and empirical drawbacks notwithstanding, is it still possible that Rawski's pattern of growth for agriculture is plausible and preferable to previous estimates? It is extremely difficult to assemble independent evidence to enable a judgement. One possible avenue to go down is to explore the calorie-intake implications of the various output estimates – though to do so creates its own problems and uncertainties. Estimates for output – and in particular for food grain output – must be consistent with the average calorie intake required to sustain the population. A contemporary China Medical Association study proposed a calorie requirement of 2,054 for a healthy diet [69]. This may be a little high but, in view of the essentially vegetarian nature of the consumption pattern, does not seem to be a serious over-statement.

The gross output of grain can be converted to its calorie availability equivalent if two coefficients are known. The first is for the proportion remaining for human consumption after seed and animal fodder requirements have been met and the second is to take account of the losses incurred in milling (de-husking). Two different sets of estimates are available (see table 6). The resulting daily calorie-intake figures, in turn, need to be supplemented by the intake from non-grain sources (again alternative coefficients are available) and from net imports (which did not exceed 2 per cent of total domestic grain output in the 1930s) [82: 155]. If Buck's coefficients are employed, all of the different output estimates back to 1914/18 emerge as plausible and give total calorie-intake figures in excess of 2,000 (unless Buck's population estimate of 592 million for the 1930s is introduced). If the lower coefficients are used, however, significant deficiencies emerge, for only the 1933 Liu and Yeh figure can be grossed up to exceed 2,000 calories and then only on the assumption of a population of 500 million. The Chang/Feuerwerker figure for the 1880s emerges as seriously deficient whichever coefficients are used.

Similarly, Rawski's estimate of a productivity gain of between 28 and 34 per cent does not easily withstand conversion into calorie-equivalent terms. Rawski's acceptance of Yeh's grain output for 1931/6 implies that an estimate for 1914/18 – and hence a calorie-intake level – can be obtained by applying the productivity gain as a deflator. It is likely that non-grain output rose more rapidly than that of grain over the period but even if per capita grain output rose by only 20 per cent this would still result in a 1914/18 calorie availability of only 1,200 to 1,325 on lower coefficients and 1,450 to 1,600 on the higher Buck figures. The implied range of total calorie intake from all sources is only 1,367 to 1,822.

As a result, either Rawski's productivity findings are too ambitious or the Yeh figure for the level of output in the 1930s is too low. If the Yeh position is correct, Rawski's conclusion on productivity growth would appear to be tenable only if the population in 1914/18 had developed the propensity to survive on a calorie intake well below that normally considered to provide an adequate diet. On the other hand, if Buck's survey results which indicate that over 90 per cent of the areas investigated had average daily consumption figures of over 1,880 calories, with only one area below 1,350, are representative and if his original higher output figures are accepted, Rawski's productivity claims become much more acceptable [68: 59]. But in this case the structure of output for the economy as a whole would emerge as even more heavily dominated by agriculture and the growth figures would need to be recalculated to take into account the higher agricultural weighting.

It is still not possible, and it may never be possible, to offer a definitive quantification of the trend experience of the Chinese economy prior to the 1950s. There is agreement that growth at the aggregate level was under way, that structural change from traditional to modern forms of production and from agricultural to industry was taking place, and that declines in average per capita income and output can be ruled out. By contrast, claims for a substantial sustained advance in average per capita incomes, for a clearly identifiable rise in per capita agricultural output and for a marked upward shift in the investment ratios – claims, in short, for the onset for modern economic growth – remain contested and contestable possibilities in their general thrust and unproven plausibilities in their detailed formulation [89: 286–295].

It is clear that the crucial deficiency in the growth-accounting analysis remains the agricultural estimates, for it appears unlikely that it will be possible to reduce the margin of error sufficiently to permit a definitive identification of the timing of the transition to modern economic growth or the extent of its progress. But it is precisely because of this limitation that the search for alternative indicators along the lines suggested by Brandt and Rawski assumes importance. The way forward, as Brandt now recognises, lies with a closer examination of the methodology and data which support these alternatives together with a fuller recognition of the heterogeneity of the agricultural experience and a more rigorous exploration of the local institutional setting and market functioning [89: 286–95]. If there were areas (the urban Treaty Port economies, Manchuria, the 'export economy' of the lower Yangzi basin and its delta, the South East Coast and, perhaps, all of the 'cores' in the macro-regions) where modern industry and/or more highly commercialised agriculture had taken hold, where markets functioned efficiently, where institutional barriers to change had been lowered and where genuine productivity gains were evident, there were others where they had not. Whatever the national outcome, the diversity of experience needs to be recognised and related to diversity in the dynamics of change.

4

Foreign trade and investment

For Mao Zedong China's modern history only began with the forced opening to more systematic foreign influence that followed the Opium War [54 vol. II: 309]. It is difficult to deny that foreign trade and investment represented powerful catalysts for change or that each continued to play a central role in China's economic modernisation. The extent, consequences and desirability of those contributions, however, remain contentious. Whatever the net effect of foreign trade and investment on the economy – and the weight of opinion has clearly moved towards a more positive outcome – it is clear that it was the product of a complex set of interactions. Trade and investment served simultaneously to stimulate and to restrain the domestic economy and to strengthen as well as to undermine the position of particular participants in that economy.

It is important to stress at the outset that the relationship between the foreign influence and China's economic modernisation should not be seen exclusively in 'impact-response' terms. An inherently dormant, stagnating China did not simply respond – or fail to respond – to a dynamic West representing the only force for change. Rather, foreign trade and investment flowed through, and became part of, an existing and evolving commercial system. Chinese merchants, producers and entrepreneurs shaped and reacted to a set of commercial opportunities and challenges – opportunities and challenges which increasingly included a foreign dimension. The availability of foreign (i.e. modern) technology may have offered the essential prerequisite for a modern industrial sector and imports and exports may have extended and intensified commercialisation within and between both urban and rural economies but they were not the sole forces for change.

The more negative view that trade and investment were one-dimensionally damaging to China can no longer be sustained. The claims that China experienced a serious net drain of resources, suffered a long-term deterioration in the terms of trade, saw her nascent modern industries oppressed by foreign competitors, found her handicraft sector destroyed by imports and was power-less to prevent agricultural producers being sucked into precarious international markets for cash crops at the expense of grain self-sufficiency have all been undermined. Even if trade and invest-ment did not fulfil the historical role of raising the equilibrium trap, the view that they had a positive and significant influence on output growth not only in the Treaty Ports but in the rural interior is gaining credence. The analysis rests in part on the level and structure of foreign trade and investment and in part on the mechanisms through which their influence, both direct and in-direct, was diffused into and through the hinterland.

The institutional framework for the build-up of foreign trade and investment in China was provided by the Unequal Treaties and the creation of the Treaty Port system. In the late eighteenth century, all trade was channelled through Canton (Guangzhou) and was handled by a specified group of Chinese merchants (the Co-hong). The first Opium War of the 1830s was fought not just to sweep aside the Chinese ban on opium imports but to formalise the 'country trade', thus widening the number of legal points of entry and increasing the range of permissible merchanting con-tents [34]. The consequence was a partial de-regulation of trade. The Treaty of Nanking (Nanjing) in 1842 established the first five Treaty Ports, ended the hong monopoly, gave foreigners residence and trading rights, and set a ceiling of 5 per cent on import duties – though in practice the rates were often higher [122: 208–10]. Subsequent treaties increased the number of open ports (to sixty-nine by 1912) and granted further concessions to foreign interests, including, for example, partial exemption from the transit (*lijin*) tax [34].

Despite this new framework, prior to the 1890s trade grew far less rapidly than merchants, manufacturers and politicians in the West had hoped for or anticipated and investment remained low, confined mainly to the facilities needed to carry on financial and merchanting activities. Two very different and, in their own terms, very successful business cultures were forced to compete and find accommodation in an environment where political and legal authority overlapped and sometimes conflicted [49: 27]. The Treaty Ports themselves were not new creations, foreigners were simply assigned concessions within existing city-ports. In Shanghai the foreign community was initially incorporated into the traditional guild (*huiguan*) organisation as another 'outsider' guild in its own designated area as a means by which its influence could be controlled and neutralised by the Chinese authorities [122: 323]. Foreigners were unfamiliar with the native language and customs (and often unwilling to learn), and this inhibited direct contact with producers and consumers in the interior.

The scale and complexity of the Chinese market and the dynamism of the Chinese commercial sector's response to the opportunities created by de-regulation were such that Western merchants were unable to operate with complete independence or displace indigenous facilities. The Western houses were forced to turn to Chinese intermediaries (compradores) to act as guarantors and tap into existing merchanting and financial networks. In the 1860s, as these Chinese compradores and merchants became familiar with, and began to adopt, Western business practices and gained access to Western financial resources and services the pace of what Hao has termed a 'commercial revolution' quickened [44: 337]. In addition, the creation of native banks (*qianzhuang*) by Ningbo merchants from Zhejiang seeking to challenge the commercial dominance of their Guangzhou rivals further facilitated the expansion of trade between Chinese and Western merchants. Foreign banks deployed their surplus funds in the form of 'chop loans' (*chaipiao*) to the native banks and native bank drafts (*zhuangpiao*) became a major form of payment in foreign trade transactions [49: 27, 31–2]. As much as 70 per cent of all Western shipping may have been financed by Chinese merchants and, whilst foreign merchants retained responsibility for importing and exporting (but then often only as commission agents), the control of the acquisition of goods for export and the distribution of imports passed almost entirely into Chinese hands [7: 36].

It was not until 1895 and the Treaty of Shimonoseki that Japan established the right of foreign nationals to operate manufacturing ventures within the Treaty Ports. This concession, together with the first tentative steps towards the creation of a railway network, led to an increased inflow of foreign capital. Imports and exports also began to grow more rapidly as China's integration into the international economy gathered momentum.

The quantitative effects of trade can be gauged through the data collected by the Imperial (later Chinese) Customs Service under Sir Robert Hart. The Customs series shows the value of recorded trade (imports and net exports) growing from about 100,000 Haiguan (Haikwan) taels annually in the mid 1860s to 200,000 by the late 1880s and surpassing 1 million during the First World War. Trade continued to increase in the 1920s and peaked at 3.24 million taels in 1931 (though the peak measured in US dollars came in 1928). On the basis of 1913 = 100 the index rose from 9.7 in 1864 to 240.7 in 1931 – representing, superficially, a twenty-fold increase in just over seventy years [115: 103]. Again, however, a cautionary gloss needs to be placed on these figures for, as they stand, they almost certainly understate the actual level of trade at any particular point in time and probably overstate the increase in trade over time. For example, junk traffic was not included and c.i.f. and f.o.b. conventions were not applied until 1904, Manchuria was excluded after the Japanese invasion in 1931 and the recorded levels do not reflect changes in the international price of silver [43: 45; 121: 8–11; 128: 199–204]. In terms of US dollars there was a more modest sixfold increase in trade between the early 1870s and the late 1920s [115: 391].

The Customs figures also reveal the changed composition of trade. On the import side, whilst opium remained the dominant item until 1890, by 1900 cotton goods took the largest single share (40 per cent). Diversification was an increasing feature of the twentieth century. By 1913 cotton goods made up only 26 per cent of imports with transportation goods, chemicals (including dyes), metals, petroleum and machinery contributing 13 per cent, and by 1931 the share of producer goods had risen to 20 per cent and exceeded that of cotton goods. On the export side, the overwhelming dominance of silk and tea (over 90 per cent in the early 1870s) was gradually eroded though, together with bean products (largely from Manchuria), they still accounted for almost

60 per cent in the early 1930s. By this time 5 per cent of exports comprised manufactured cotton goods and over one-third of all exports were accounted for by categories which individually contributed less than 3 per cent to the total [43: 50–2; 53: 103–7; 121: 17].

Silk was of particular importance. In the eighteenth century the main export destination was South America via Manila – hence the inflow of Spanish silver dollars. Trade with Europe and the US gathered pace after the end of the East India Company monopoly in 1833 and was further stimulated by the creation of the Treaty Ports, with Shanghai quickly emerging as the main export conduit. In the late 1860s France became a major purchaser and exports rose again. Raw (reeled) silk exports rose from an average of 25 million taels (62,000 piculs) in 1870–4 to 141 million taels (173,000 piculs) by 1925–9 whilst fabric exports increased from 2.3 million taels (5,000 piculs) to 29 million taels (33,000 piculs). Fabric exports peak at 28 per cent of the total in 1888 (though they rose again to 41 per cent in the depression year of 1934). In the late nineteenth century, silk exports exceeded those of tea and accounted for between 30 and 40 per cent of all exports. With domestic demand in decline, the industry became increasingly export orientated. More than half of output may have been exported by the 1880s, perhaps three-quarters by the mid-1920s. Over the period as a whole, earnings from silk were almost sufficient to finance the whole of China's importation of cotton yarn and cloth. There is little doubt that the expansion of exports could have been even greater. If quality control had been improved, China could have claimed part of the world market that went to Japan; though if it had, the distress in the 1930s when the depression hit would have been even greater [108: 65–76, 82–4, 197–8].

Estimates of the relationship between total trade and national income remain tentative and subject to a significant margin of error. In the 1880s the average recorded levels of trade represent 5 per cent of the Feuerwerker/Chang estimate for GDP [41]. Feuerwerker has advanced a figure of 7 per cent for 1933 and 10 per cent for the late 1920s, and Dernberger an over-optimistic average of 17 per cent for the 1920s [53: 99; 117: 27n]. Comparing the peak trade values for 1931 with Yeh's recent GDP estimate for the same year (both at 1933 prices and exchange rates) gives a figure of 10.2 per cent. These levels are not abnormally low in comparison to other large and essentially self-sufficient economies and those wishing to play down the quantitative importance of trade have turned towards the extremely low level of trade on a per capita basis (US $1.6 in both 1914 and 1931) with China appearing at the bottom of the list of the eighty-three countries for which League of Nations data were collected in 1912 [53: 50]. Foreign investment in China was also relatively low by international standards, particularly in per capita terms. Remer's figures show investment doubling between 1902 and 1914 and doubling again by 1931. Even so, cumulative investment reached only US $3,243 million in 1931, representing no more than one-third of GDP for that year and less than US $7 per capita [129: 117].

Until the early nineteenth century the pattern of China's external trade appears more akin to that of an advanced economy – exports of manufactured or processed goods (silk, porcelain, tea, etc.) were exchanged for barely processed goods (opium). Imported manufactured goods made little headway; they were either uncompetitive in terms of quality and price (cotton goods), irrelevant (cutlery, pianos, etc.), or unaffordable to the vast majority of the population. The balance of trade which had remained in China's favour throughout the eighteenth century was only temporarily disrupted by the rise in opium imports, for the Customs figures reveal a surplus again in the late 1860s. Despite the continuation of opium imports and the efforts by foreign merchants to penetrate the China market, this position was maintained until the 1890s when a growing deficit in manufactured goods pushed the merchandise account into the red. China's trading position subsequently typified that of an underdeveloped economy. Yet, whilst only about three-quarters of total imports were financed by exports, the deficits did not exceed 2 per cent of national income [114: 395].

The fragmentary evidence available on the capital side of the account suggests that the annual repatriation of profits exceeded the inflow of new funds. The continued deficits on the merchandise and investment accounts, however, were not financed by the export of gold and silver, at least until the 1930s. Rather, they were financed by income from service transactions and remit-

tances from overseas Chinese. China continued to experience a
net inflow of silver [114: 401].

Nor was there any long-term deterioration in the terms of trade
(measured in terms of import and export prices). The adjusted
Nankai figures show a rising, if fluctuating, trend prior to 1930.
An improvement of 25 per cent between the early 1870s and 1913
was followed by a deterioration during the wartime period and a
revival in the 1920s (to regain the 1913 level). The depression
brought a sharp decline, though the position remained more
favourable than that of 1918 [121: 57].

In aggregate terms, therefore, China's external trade remained
modest, though not insignificant in relation to the economy as a
whole and, despite deficits on the merchandise and investment
accounts, there seems to have been no serious or persistent drain
of resources. If anything, prior to the 1930s, China benefited from
an improving trend in the terms of trade and a net inflow of specie.
Moreover, this trade and investment, the modern technology,
methods and ideas which they embodied, and the incomes which
they generated were heavily concentrated geographically in favour
of the Treaty Ports and Southern Manchuria.

Foreign trade was channelled through a small number of ports
and, in particular, Shanghai. In 1931, twenty ports accounted for
almost 80 per cent of recorded trade. Shanghai took over 70 per
cent in the early 1870s and retained almost 50 per cent in 1931. A
similar position holds for investment. Shanghai's share increased
over time to reach 34 per cent in 1931 (43 per cent of all
investment which can be geographically identified) [53]. If the
ports taken together accounted for 20 per cent of GDP in 1931 (it
is unlikely to have been any more), the value of trade throughput
was equivalent to one half of the value of their contribution to
national income and, if they were responsible for only 10 per cent,
the two would have been of the same order of magnitude. If
Shanghai's contribution to GDP were no more than 5 per cent
then the value of its foreign trade turnover would still have
equalled its contribution to value-added in national income.
Similarly, if Shanghai's population had not exceeded 3 million by
the early 1930s each resident, on average, would have attracted
more than US $1,000 in foreign investment [55: 265–6].

Whether or not China could have produced her own industrial

revolution in the late eighteenth and early nineteenth centuries, once the crucial technological breakthroughs had been made in Europe the availability of that technology became the catalyst for the creation of a modern sector in China and foreign investment in that technology remained central to its subsequent development. Although some enterprises deploying Western technology were founded in the decades following the Opium Wars it was the new treaty rights of 1895 which opened the way for direct foreign investment and the rapid expansion of modern industry, largely, but not exclusively, in the Treaty Port areas. Yet neither the particular dispersion of modern industry nor the sectoral concentration on consumer goods that emerged within it were simply the product of foreign domination. Rather, they resulted from the natural market-orientated (i.e. cost-price) advantages and demand realities of the time [92: 79, 92]. And unless this expansion took place at the expense of existing handicraft or other non-mechanical production – and on the whole it did not – it must have represented a net increase in national output.

Nor did foreign enterprises establish themselves to the exclusion of Chinese concerns. Within the factory sector, Chinese producers, by the 1930s, dominated in terms of employment (70 per cent) and output (two-thirds of Gross Value of Output (GVO), and 80 per cent in China proper) though not in terms of capitalisation (37 per cent) [53: 35–7]. And the available evidence on profitability and productivity does not indicate foreign oppression [97]. In general, foreign investment provided a net increase in output and incomes and offered an important demonstration effect. Although foreign concerns possessed certain inherent advantages, so too did Chinese producers. Chinese employees in Western-owned ventures also learned skills which they could subsequently deploy on their own behalf and the foreign and international settlements provided a safe and more conducive environment within which Chinese business could prosper. Chinese enterprises largely catered for the domestic consumption market but also came to serve foreign industry – hence the emergence of an indigenous producer good capacity [102]. Without the Japanese occupation of, and investment in, Manchuria it is unlikely that a heavy industrial base would have been created in the 1930s and 1940s, although the social, military, political and psychological costs of that control were enormous [175; 176; 177; 178].

If, therefore, foreign trade and investment remained small they were not insignificant in relation to the Chinese economy as a whole, and their geographical concentration ensured that they played a central role in the creation of a modern urban industrial sector in the Treaty Ports and South Manchuria. But how did they impinge on the experience of the rural economy? If China is seen as a dual economy with a modern dynamic coastal economy transposed against an isolated, stagnant rural interior then it follows that foreign trade and investment had little influence on the latter – except, perhaps, in a negative sense.

On the face of it this position has some credibility. Little foreign capital was directed towards agriculture. Investment in transportation (railways and shipping) did serve to increase market integration, although even in 1937 only just over 20,000 kilometres of railway were in operation and less than 12,000 kilometres in China Proper [92]. Foreign investment could not, and did not seek to, transform or even significantly change the underlying technology. Moreover, the level of agricultural exports and imports remained small in relation to total output. It is unlikely that farm output destined for export exceeded 5 per cent of total production or that imports (mainly rice) exceeded 3 per cent. Most imports catered for the Treaty Port market and did not compete directly with the products of handicraft industry [91: 121].

But if Rawski and Brandt are correct and growth was evident in the agricultural sector and, perhaps, in the rural economy as a whole, can it be shown that foreign trade and investment influenced the rural economy in ways which are consistent with, or which might have promoted, that growth? An examination of the structure of trade and of the mechanisms through which the influence of China's increased involvement in the international economy were transmitted suggest that they can.

For certain products and, therefore, for certain areas the level of additional demand which exports generated was large enough to influence the level and pattern of output. Soya beans became a staple export crop in Manchuria and the buoyant demand for silk products prior to 1930 encouraged large numbers of peasant farmers to plant mulberry trees and turn to silk-worm rearing in Jiangsu and Guangdong. In addition, the growth of modern industry, a growth for which foreign trade and investment were partly responsible, increased the demand for agricultural raw materials (principally cotton but also tobacco and oil seed) and for marketed grain and other foodstuffs. Foreign trade and investment served, directly and indirectly, to increase the level of demand and intensify the commercialisation of agriculture. They provided opportunities for farmers to alter the pattern of cultivation in favour of higher-yielding crops, to increase the value of output and to increase (or at least protect) their incomes. Yet care has to be taken not to press the point too far. The acreage devoted to commercial crops probably did not exceed 10 per cent of the total [82: 11] (though if marketed grain and vegetables are included the proportion would be much higher) and, as Faure has shown, only rarely was the conversion to commercial crops taken so far as to undermine local self-sufficiency in food production [73].

Turning to the effect of foreign trade and investment on rural handicraft industries, a far less pessimistic view than was once prevalent is also revealed. These issues are dealt with in more detail in the next chapter but some of the main conclusions are relevant here. The subject is a complex one because competition in the interior was felt through imports, foreign investment in modern capacity in the Treaty Ports and the parallel investment by Chinese manufacturers, and it is not always possible to separate the effects. Moreover, many Chinese consumers did not distinguish between modern and foreign goods – all modern goods were regarded as 'foreign'. In 1930, 131 'foreign' goods were on sale in Xunwu in Jiangxi province though less than ten were genuine imports [87: 69–70]. Whilst Feuerwerker [53: 34] is right to point out that 'anyone who would claim that the Hunan or Szechwan [Sichuan] peasant in the 1930s dressed in Naigaiwata cotton, smoked BAT cigarettes and used Meiji sugar has a big case to prove', the diffusion of 'modern' if not 'foreign' goods may have penetrated the countryside more deeply than is sometimes realised. Xunwu is a case in point. Not only were modern goods finding their way into an area which, even in the 1990s, is still difficult for foreigners to reach, but the presence of those goods in other adjacent areas to which local producers had traditionally exported was causing concern to the Xunwu merchant community [87: 65]. Similarly, if grain could be drawn out of the whole of the Yangzi drainage system manufactured goods could be taken in. Furthermore, modern textile goods had reached villages some distance from Kunming in the far southwest and remote areas in Shaanxi in the north and were displacing, or had displaced, local handicraft products by the late 1930s [74: 243; 151: 106].

Cotton textiles are normally taken as the litmus test for the competitive pressures on handicraft producers. Native producers both within the household and in workshops did experience competition from cheap imported machine-spun yarn in the late nineteenth century and their output fell. However, it was probably competition from the modern sector in China itself rather than imports which posed the greater threat. Even so, whilst hand-spinning was permanently reduced it did not disappear and the availability of machine yarn, together with rising per capita consumption of cloth, helped the handloom weaving sector to continue to expand until the late 1920s. It seems extremely unlikely that the value of handicraft output as a whole fell before the 1930s, unlikely that it rose any less rapidly than the rate of growth of population, but unlikely that it expanded any more rapidly than population (see chapter 5).

In addition to the demand and supply consequences of foreign trade and investment it is also necessary to consider the monetary influences that stemmed from China's greater involvement in the international economy. Neither the increased level of imports and exports nor foreign investment in modern industry created commercialisation, but they did help to propel an existing commercialised system forward. The more open and integrated markets were, and the more nearly perfectly competitive those markets, the more rapidly and the more widely any internationally induced price effects would be communicated and felt.

For Brandt, a significant element in the increasing agricultural price integration with world markets derived from China's role in the Asian monsoon rice trade. The southern province of Guangdong had long been a rice-deficit province. By the eighteenth century the demand was supplied from the neighbouring Guangxi and this was subsequently augmented by the long-distance movement of rice from Hunan in central China. Rice was drawn down the Yangzi to distribution centres in the delta and then sent by coastal junks to Guangzhou, the chief port in Guangdong. With the advent of sea-going steam ships, the shipment costs from Hunan were no longer lower than those from South East Asia and, by the end of the nineteenth century, south China was absorbing substantial rice imports. Because her share of the trade was small, China became a price-taker on international markets and Chinese producers were forced to match import prices – not just in Guangdong but, via Shanghai, in the Middle Yangzi. By the end of the nineteenth century, prices in Guangdong were no longer being set internally and by 1912 this was also true of Shanghai – even though Shanghai still imported little, if any, Asian rice. Not only can close price correlations be observed between price movements in south China (and later Shanghai) and Siam, Burma, India and Saigon but those correlations are seen to rise over time [67: 40–51; 174]. Moreover, high correlation coefficients are evident between prices in Shanghai and the rice ports on the Yangzi with variations a function of distance from Shanghai. Shanghai's need to remain competitive in the Guangdong market ensured that imports became an important influence on Shanghai's own prices and throughout the catchment area that served it. For Brandt, the existence of large numbers of peasant producers and large numbers of merchants kept markets highly competitive and explains the high degree of market and price integration across and between macro-regions [67: 58].

But other, monetary, influences were also at work on prices. China remained on a silver standard until the mid 1930s and, as a result, experienced a long-term depreciation in its currency and a tendency for prices to rise (at least until 1930) [73: 64–83]. Depreciation, however, was not the only factor at work. Between 1872 and 1930 the notional silver Haiguan tael depreciated against sterling by 76 per cent whilst the price of rice in Shanghai rose by 467 per cent [67: 44–6]. Moreover, when the international value of silver rose rapidly during the First World War prices in China did not adjust downwards. A second monetary influence came through the import of silver. These flows augmented the money supply and contributed towards the general upward movement in prices, particularly in the late 1920s. A third factor was the debasement of the coinage and a rise in the rate of exchange between copper and silver. Although primarily a domestic mechanism, it was facilitated by the establishment of foreign mints which transformed the coinage supply in the late 1890s. According to Faure it was the abrupt shifts in the exchange rate in favour of copper which account for the major price changes prior to 1912 [73: 72–4].

Just as external influences contributed to the deflation of the early nineteenth century so they also served to underwrite price rises from the aftermath of the Taiping Rebellion to 1930. In this latter period the farming community faced a favourable combination of rising internal and international demand, rising internal prices, a move in the terms of trade in its favour (both internally and externally) and a protected international competitiveness brought about by currency depreciation. Farmers producing for export probably gained most but all were able to take advantage of the beneficial trends. It was this combination which, according to Brandt and Rawski, promoted productivity and welfare gains in the agricultural sector [67: 169–74; 92].

But the more integrated the internal markets were and the more producers gained from a combination of currency depreciation and silver imports prior to 1930, the more China stood to lose during the following decade when the international depression began to bite. The demand for bean products and silk fell away dramatically and the economic expansion was checked. Silver appreciated as other economies came off the gold standard and silver began to flow out – rapidly once the US silver-purchase scheme became operational. As silver was drawn out of the countryside and, as demand dropped, prices fell [55; 67; 73]. The extent, rapidity and generality of the price falls provide a further indication that much of the hinterland was highly integrated with the more urbanised sea-board and with the international economy.

In the Treaty Ports, the inflow of international currency in exchange for silver laid the basis for an increase in the money supply and the adoption of a managed currency [55: 264]. The downward price spiral was slowed and then reversed. Yeh's figures suggest that factory output continued to rise in each successive year of the depression whilst the gross value of output generated in construction, the utilities, modern transport and finance either remained stable or rose [94: 97]. But in the countryside there were neither the financial institutions to issue notes nor the willingness on the part of the public to accept them and the consequences were far more serious. Prices fell rapidly (by up to 59 per cent) and the terms of trade moved sharply against the farmer [51: 184].

Yet, in an aggregate sense, the downturn appears less marked than might be expected. The gross value of agricultural output fell by under 1 per cent in 1933, by less than 12 per cent in the following year and then recovered to exceed the previous peak by 1936 [94: 97]. Nor can all the difficulties be placed at the door of foreign trade and investment. Climatic conditions were particularly unfavourable in the early 1930s and handicraft producers in the north were affected by the loss of traditional markets in Manchuria after the Japanese invasion in 1931. In the case of the hard-hit silk-worm farmers in the south, the real problem may have been population pressure. By the early twentieth century the downward pressure on farm size had reached the point where it was difficult, if not impossible, to reach subsistence (after rent and taxes) from traditional grain farming alone in many areas in Jiangsu and Guangdong. For two or three decades, perhaps more, buoyant international demand had disguised the problem and provided a respite. In the 1930s when the favourable external influences were put into reverse the safety valve was removed. A return to subsistence farming in the face of increased rents and a heightened tax burden was no longer an option and China's own urban markets were not always strong enough to provide the necessary relief [64: 224].

5

Industry: traditional and modern

The combination of the so-called 'second industrial revolution' of the Song (960–1279) and the emergence of a commodity economy had served to extend China's early technological leadership and provide a means by which industrial output could keep pace with population growth without significant further adjustment. In the wake of this leadership the improved co-ordination of an increasing number of small-scale units through market mechanisms enabled output to continue to increase, though the corollary was a five-century technological stagnation [106: 167]. Even in the eighteenth century when population almost doubled and industrial output probably grew at an unprecedented rate, the technological base did not advance. Although there were large-scale industrial undertakings representing substantial concentrations of capital in, for example, ceramics, iron-making, salt extraction and copper mining, although large silk and cotton weaving workshops figured more prominently and although isolated technological advances were still evident, the bulk of output continued to be generated in small specialist workshops or individual households employing technology very little different from that of the Song [142]. The early technological innovation had given way to persistent inertia.

In conditions of declining farm size, increasingly efficient market mechanisms and substantial seasonal agricultural labour underutilization, rural industry had expanded and, by the eighteenth century, may have become geographically more generalised than in Europe[1: 24–5; 15: 42]. Consumerism was embedded in the structure of society and was the product of a fluid and often ambiguous social structure in which the pursuit of wealth and status encouraged product differentiation. Handicraft producers largely, but not exclusively, operating in a rural environment faced a 'consumer continuum' consisting of a few very rich people, many of middling wealth and a majority who were poor. The emergence and proliferation of 'brand names' across a range of trades including cotton, tea, scissors and medicine as a marketing strategy designed to engender a national, rather than a simply local, appeal is one example of the sophistication of China's commodity economy [35: 266–8].

However, the early Qing era can be seen as the apogee of the strength and vitality of the traditional system and the commercialised rural industrialisation which, in many ways, resembled European proto-industrialisation, did not generate (and was not accompanied by) the transition into factory-based production. Silk and cotton technology in China may still have been more advanced than in Japan or Britain in the 1740s but, as Faure points out, 'the handicraft workshop was neither a capitalist institution nor set upon a course which might turn into one' [7: 6]. A high pre-modern technological threshold and advanced consumerism did not 'sprout' into commercial or industrial capitalism. Smithian dynamics remained in place [15: 62].

The reasons for this technological inertia lie in a complex amalgam of political, social, cultural and economic factors but, in essence, it persisted because change was not necessary or perceived as desirable. The continued availability of factors of production in the context of open, competitive and (in the eighteenth century) increasingly privatised market conditions enabled industrial output to advance unimpeded and China was still probably more successful in accommodating rising population without significant strain than Europe. The distinctive Confucian political economy which was designed to perpetuate an expanding agrarian empire remained intact. The aim continued to be to return to the 'golden ages' of the Song or Ming rather than look beyond them. China had seen the past and it worked: it was not just that there was no need to change, change was unthinkable [7; 8; 15; 142].

Yet, although that vision was no longer appropriate in the changed conditions of the nineteenth century, when it was necessary to contend not just with heightened Malthusian boundaries but with a superior Western technology, for the next century and a half the rural economy continued to operate within essentially the same Smithian dynamics and it managed to hold both pressures at bay. The intensified commercialisation of crop production, the greater integration of proto-industrial production and the spread of best (traditional) practice continued to offer the means by which population growth could continue to be accommodated without any serious long-term downward trend in family incomes and without the technological or organisational transformation of rural industry. If anything, population pressure contributed to the supply-side dynamics and small-scale rural industry retained a quantitatively important role in the economy. Proto-industrialisation continued without giving rise to, or succumbing to, industrial capitalism. Competition from modern industry, both foreign and indigenous, had its effect but it was by no means exclusively negative. The incorporation of low-level modern technology within rural industry, for example, could serve to strengthen its ability to survive [6; 15].

At the same time there is little doubt that more fundamental change in the level and form of industrial output and, in particular, the rise of modern industry was inhibited by the generally low level of average incomes and by a number of elements inherent in the traditional political economy. And these long-standing ideas, attitudes and practices took time to be broken down. Confucian susceptibilities which had viewed uncontrolled industrial expansion as potentially disruptive and subversive, and anxieties over the social consequences of the excessive pursuit of profit (which inhibited the formation of concentrations of mercantile wealth), for example, now acted as obstacles to the transition to industrial capitalism in general and the formation of modern industry in particular [15: 150]. Some features proved incompatible with the new forms of production and had to be abandoned, but others were maintained or adjusted and eventually came to underwrite and condition the rise of a distinctive indigenous industrial response. A new, more scientific, education system was required; mechanisms to generate the resources to finance an advance into significantly different (and more expensive) technology had to be created; and Western ideas needed to be assimilated into existing accounting and managerial practices. The Confucian heritage was not ultimately inimical to these developments but, inevitably, it took time for the adjustments to be made, particularly if they were to emerge in a way which grew out of the tradition rather than in a way which simply rejected it.

As these features were put in place and as modern technology was introduced new industries were gradually created – cigarettes, electricity, engineering, matches, rubber. Others came to operate on a totally new scale (coal mining, iron and steel) and in some cases a modern component was added which supplemented, stimulated and/or undermined existing production (silk, cotton textiles, flour milling, etc.). A modern urban industrial sector was generated and even if it remained qualitatively largely distinct and separate from its traditional small-scale rural counterpart the relationship between the two is an analytically important one. Moreover, if the focus of analysis tends to shift towards the former it should always be remembered that the latter, though in relative decline, remained quantitatively the more significant throughout the pre-Communist era [4; 5; 15].

Where it came into contact with modern industry, the survival of the small-scale rural sector was increasingly dependent on its ability to compete on grounds of price and quality and, in some cases, on the persistence of a discrete demand for the traditional product. These processes are most evident in cotton textiles – the classic example of the confrontation between modern and traditional methods of production.

Textile production and distribution were already heavily commercialised by the early eighteenth century. Certain cotton-growing areas (Hebei/Shandong and Jiangsu) had developed strong handicraft sectors and supplied markets throughout the empire [76: 67]. Producers within both the household and rural and urban workshops functioned directly in a market context – a putting-out system had not taken hold. As imports rose and modern mills were established in China in the nineteenth century, handicraft suppliers found their position challenged. Competition in the spinning branch proved the more severe and here the decline preceded that in weaving.

The essential difference between the experience of the two sectors arises from the productivity gap between modern and traditional methods of production. In spinning, the efficiency differential between power-driven material and the single hand-

Table 8. Cotton-textile output 1870–1936

	1871/80	1901/10A	1901/10B	1905/9	1924/7	1925/7	1931/6	1932/6	1934/6
Yarn supply 1870–1936 (in lbs.)									
Machine-spun	0	133	183	174	822	947	1,202	948	1,200
Hand-spun	653	840	378	551	409	587	422	340	413
Total output	653	973	561	125	1,231	1,534	1,642	1,288	1,613
Hand-spun share (%)	100	86	67	76	33	33	26	26	26
Imports share (%)	2	33	38	—	—	7	8	—	1
Cloth supply 1870–1936 (in sq. yds.)									
Power loom	0	24	56	58	433	440	1,249	1,147	1,260
Hand loom	1,612	1,850	2,013	1,876	2,845	3,630	2,480	2,260	2,880
Total output	1,612	1,874	2,069	1,934	3,278	3,970	3,729	3,407	4,140
Handloom share (%)	100	99	97	97	87	89	67	66	70
Imports share (%)	23	35	—	—	—	18	—	—	8

Sources: 1871/80, 1901/10 [43].

1905/9, 1924/7, 1932/6 [97: 232–5]. Chao's yarn figures have been converted to lbs. at the rate of 1 bale = 467 lbs. Chao cites a figure of only 13 million lbs. for yarn imports 1905/9 which seems unrealistically low. The average from Hsiao is 309 million lbs. [111]. Any increase in the supply should raise the cloth output proportionately.

1925/7, 1934/6 [101, tables II.9, V.2]. Piculs have been converted to lbs. at the rate of 1 picul = 133.33 lbs.

1931/6 [92].

spinner was enormous (as much as 400 to 1). For weaving the gap was much smaller, particularly when domestic producers acquired metal-framed handlooms themselves. The comparative advantage lay with weaving or, rather, the comparative disadvantage lay with spinning. It made sense to purchase machine yarn and concentrate on weaving. By the early 1920s only one-third of domestic yarn production emanated from the hand-spinners and by the 1930s only a quarter. Handloom cloth, by contrast, still captured almost 90 per cent of the market in the 1920s and at least two-thirds in the 1930s. Handicraft weaving probably reached its peak in the late 1920s at a level double that of the 1870s (see table 8).

If the eventual decline in handicraft production was inevitable, two more difficult issues remain. Why, given the overwhelming technological superiority of machine spinning, should *any* hand-spinning have survived and why did the bulk of surviving household production continue to take place on un-modernised single-spindle devices and narrow looms? Part of the answer to the latter question derives from the nature of the production unit itself – the family. Multi-spindle machines had been available in China for centuries but remained a rarity. The restraint, according to Chao, was that although more efficient they required the attention of two or more family members working together, and this was seldom practicable. Similarly, teamwork was required for the production of wide or patterned cloth and it was for this reason that the single-operative Jacquard loom gained ground so quickly after its introduction in 1906 [97: 64–75].

At the broader level, because all hand-spun yarn was consumed by handloom weavers the fortunes of both sectors were dependent on the ability of the weaver to compete in the market, on the activities of a supportive merchanting community and on the natural protection given by a persistent demand for the handicraft product. Competition was effected by reducing labour costs, by utilising the products of the modern sector (cheap machine-spun yarn) and by incorporating low-level modern technology (iron-framed broad-looms). Whereas in the modern sector subsistence wages needed to be paid (though the bulk of the workforce was female and the subsistence wage was very low), in the handicraft sector this requirement did not operate. For many families additional income for non-farming activities was critical for their survival. The opportunity cost of much household labour in the off-farm seasons was low. For the old and young and, perhaps, for most women it was virtually zero. It was not just that footbinding made it difficult for women to work in the fields. The propagation by the early Qing of a 'men work and women weave' division, with its strong moral and social disapproval for women who worked outside the household, had a lasting effect [109: 90–1]. Any income was better than none, and though the return on hand-spinning failed to cover even minimum food requirements it could still serve as the most effective way of supplementing the family income. A similar principle applied to weaving, though here the skill input was greater and the rate of return higher [97; 105; 107; 110; 111].

Yet the very low cost of labour in the handicraft sector cannot, in itself, provide a complete explanation for the survival of the industry, for handicraft cloth was still more expensive than its machine-made counterpart implying that there existed distinct demand schedules. Much (though by no means all) of the urban demand was lost to the machine product, even amongst the poor – modern cloth was becoming more acceptable, perhaps even fashionable, and it was cheaper. But in the countryside demand remained overwhelmingly for the traditional handwoven product. The use of hand-spun yarn (even if only as the weft) ensured that the cloth was heavier, warmer and more durable. And traditional peasant outfits were (and still are) designed and cut to the dimensions of the narrower cloth. Nor should it be taken for granted that handloom cloth was a standard, coarse, product. A substantial variety of texture and design was possible on handlooms. An eighteenth-century observer suggested that cotton cloth produced in Jiangnan just south of the mouth of the Yangzi was 'like the nap on the wool blanket the emperor used for ancestral worship' [109: 85–6]. Weavers were highly skilled and could cater for the specific requirements of ethnic minorities or individual villages in ways that producers in Shanghai or Tianjin could not. Cloth produced on traditional wooden-framed looms or on unpowered iron-framed looms in rural workshops using a combination of hand- and machine-spun yarn could still find a niche in commercial markets, particularly where there was support from a local merchanting community. In addition, it is important to recognise that most handwoven cloth was produced within the household for its own consumption [111: 38]. If the opportunity cost of labour was low, if the family had little or no disposable income or had limited access to the market, it made perfect economic sense to satisfy its own consumption requirements at minimum cost.

Whether the additional employment opportunities created in weaving offset the contraction of hand-spinning or whether the income gains in one compensated for the losses in the other is unclear. If the value of handicraft output did not fall in aggregate terms the income must have been spread more thinly as population rose. But if consumption and output outstripped population, as Rawski suggests, there could have been net gains. The net effect may have been an employment loss but an income gain. According to Brandt there was a reduction of 25 to 30 per cent in the labour input between the 1870s and the 1930s, whilst total value added rose by at least 10 to 15 per cent, implying gains in the value of the labour day of 40 to 50 per cent [67: 124–30].

So why then did the handicraft-weaving sector decline in the 1930s? The supply-side factors remained in place and, as the depression began to permeate the rural economy, wage levels fell even further. Rather, the constraints were on the demand side. If handloom cloth was regarded as a superior – though more expensive – product, the relative prosperity of the agricultural sector in the 1920s would have allowed that preference to be satisfied. In the 1930s peasants were, increasingly, forced to settle for 'inferior' lightweight cloth because that was all they could now afford. And the important Manchurian market was lost in the wake of the Japanese invasion in 1931. Yet handicraft spinning and weaving remained remarkably resilient in the face of adversity and probably expanded again in the 1940s as wartime disturbances disrupted supplies from the modern sector. What may have finally undermined independent household and workshop production were the restrictions placed on the markets for raw cotton and finished cloth by the new Communist government in the early 1950s. It was the movement to collectivise agriculture rather than foreign competition or the rise of a modern sector in China which forced the virtual elimination of traditional handicraft production [105: 197–9].

If cotton-textile producers were confronted by competitive

imports, limited export prospects and an expanding domestic market, their counterparts in silk faced no import threat, a large and expansionary international demand, but a home market that displayed no long-term growth. The industry reorientated geographically after the Taiping disruption and began to be transformed technologically in the 1890s through the adoption of steam filature reeling and the introduction of iron-framed looms in workshops and power looms in factories. These moves led to the separation of reeling and weaving from sericulture itself and, as with cotton, it was the first of these handicraft stages which was most vulnerable. Hand-reeling in the household and in workshops not only claimed a declining proportion of expanding export volumes and values, but fell in absolute terms. By contrast, hand-weaving probably increased because mechanisation spread more slowly. In some of the older silk areas, such as Sichuan and Zhejiang, where the focus remained on high-quality specialist production, hand-spinning and weaving continued to dominate even in the 1920s but in others filature silk took over. In Jiangsu, production came to be concentrated in the cities (particularly Shanghai and Wuxi) though in Guangdong spinning and weaving were located in the cocoon-producing areas themselves. Buoyant international demand ensured that margins remained relatively high until the late nineteenth century and it is likely that downward pressure on rates of return to labour was less serious than in the case of cotton. Modern technology could bring a reduction in risk and guarantee a consistent quality but it could not improve on the quality of the best hand produced silk. Again, handicraft production could survive where it was close to cocoon supplies, where producers were sensitive to changing demands and where rates of return on (mainly female and child) labour could be reduced [108].

The existence of separate demand schedules, the ability to reduce labour costs, the ability of the handicraft sector to strengthen itself by absorbing low-level modern technology – what Elvin terms 'pre-modern over development' – ensured that modern production, in general, served to supplement rather than replace that of the traditional sector [6]. To make significant headway, modern industry required not just the availability of new technology but entrepreneurship and supplies of capital. The commercial revolution of the middle of the nineteenth century in conjunction with the government's incursion into modern military technology provided a limited if tentative initiative. The momentum was extended through 'government sponsored-merchant management' enterprises but, until the 1890s, the size of the modern sector remained negligible.

Subsequent growth was rapid and by the late 1930s modern industry occupied a more significant, though still modest place in the economy. Whilst the rate of growth is impressive (an average in excess of 8 per cent per annum for the twenty-five years from 1912 to 1936) and stands comparison with other economies in the early stages of their industrialisation, modern manufacturing industry (defined as enterprises using mechanical power and with more than thirty employees) still accounted for less than 3 per cent of GNP by the late 1930s [92; 96]. Even if modern mining and the utilities are included the modern contribution did not reach 5 per cent at a time when handicrafts still contributed more than 7 per cent [92: 72; 94: 97]. The rise of modern industry largely remained a 'regional phenomenon' and was biased heavily towards consumer goods. Although China was a major international producer of cotton textiles and Shanghai consumed more electricity than Manchester or Birmingham by the late 1920s, in other areas there were substantial shortfalls [55].

Feuerwerker has estimated that at least 549 Chinese-owned private and semi-official modern mining and manufacturing enterprises had been established by 1913. In addition, 96 foreign-owned and 40 Sino-foreign ventures had been formed, with a capital almost matching that of the Chinese sector [43]. The First World War stimulated rapid increases in output, though the major increases in productive capacity came only after hostilities in Europe had ceased and the new plant and equipment could be delivered. Between 1914 and 1922, modern textile capacity trebled (spindle capacity reached 3.6 million) and China became the most rapidly expanding producer in the world [96: 301–6]. Coal output from modern mines increased from 5 to 13 million tons [103: 10]. The adjustment to this 'golden age' as new capacity became operational and competitive pressures mounted was short-lived and, in the mid-1920s, the momentum was regained, helped by a series of foreign trade boycotts fuelled by rising Chinese nationalism. By 1933 over 3,800 factories were operational with a capitalisation of Ch$2,186m. Of the under-takings, 822 were Chinese, 65 per cent of the capital was Chinese and they gave employment to perhaps a million workers [53: 18]. In aggregate terms this expansion was slowed but not reversed by the effects of the international depression (both internal and external). Whilst individual sectors faltered others continued to expand [94]. Tariff protection, currency depreciation prior to 1931, a continued expansion of the money supply and increased Japanese investment in Manchuria all underwrote the continued buoyancy [92; 50].

After 1937 and the onset of the Sino-Japanese war the picture is less clear. In Free China (the fourteen provinces controlled by the Nationalist Government) output rose as capacity was shipped westwards from Shanghai and other centres of modern industry and as the area was forced to become self-sufficient [136]. Little research has been done on output trends in the area occupied by the Japanese (the Eastern seaboard as far south as Guangzhou and Hong Kong, the lower Yangzi and large parts of the North China plain). If industrial output rose in the North, Shanghai suffered badly [53: 23–5]. In Manchuria under Japanese control output increased rapidly at least until 1941. In the 1920s, growth in Manchuria, as a frontier economy, still centred on agriculture and, in particular, on the export of staple crops such as soya beans. The area was badly affected by the depression and in the 1930s the economy was integrated into the Japanese Empire and reorientated around heavy industry [175; 176; 178]. The planned targets of forced industrialisation were not met, however, and the expected benefit to Japan had not materialised by the time of Pearl Harbor. The subsequent disruption of the flow of investment and essential raw materials made it difficult to secure further increases in output. The onset of civil war after 1945 did nothing to create the conditions of stability that were necessary for industry to flourish or even recover either in Manchuria or China Proper and in 1949 output levels were still below their pre-war peaks.

Manufacturing output was heavily concentrated in the coastal provinces and particular key-ports – areas which possessed the greatest commercial and strategic advantages. The coastal provinces, and particularly Liaoning in Manchuria and Jiangsu at the mouth of the Yangzi, contributed almost two-thirds of output.

Within this the three ports of Shanghai, Tianjin and Qingdao dominated textile production and Shanghai alone provided 40 per cent of all modern manufacturing output. Manchuria with 8 or 9 per cent of the population contributed 14 per cent of manufacturing output in 1933 [53: 80]. Yet, within the Chinese modern sector some geographical diversification was underway. Much of the expansion in cotton-textile capacity took place outside Shanghai and the interior cities – for example Chengdu in Sichuan – were beginning to build a modern capability even before the Japanese invasion.

Although modern industry taken as a whole was heavily orientated to consumer goods, producer goods were growing in relative importance. By 1933 chemicals, non-metallic minerals, basic metals and metal products accounted for 15 per cent of manufacturing output and 22 per cent of value-added [53]. There was a growing engineering sector and, through a 'learning by doing' process, indigenous concerns were able to service existing machinery and provide new plant and equipment [102]. In the 1930s heavy industry was promoted vigorously by the government. In 1932, as the creation of a planned national defence economy became a priority, the secret National Defence Commission was established and the plans which emanated from this body sought to ensure the strategic development of state-run heavy industries and mines in a new 'economic centre' in the less vulnerable interior [138: 78–95].

Outside Manchuria the bulk of output continued to be generated in Chinese-owned enterprises. In only one sector (lumber) did foreign-owned output exceed Chinese and the Chinese dominance in the share of both output and employment was most pronounced in the producers' goods sector. At first sight the fact that the Chinese share of the number of enterprises exceeded its share of output and (by an even wider margin) of capitalisation suggests a preponderance of smaller, more highly labour-intensive undertakings within the Chinese sector [53: 35–7]. This probably was the case though capitalisation is not an entirely accurate indicator of size. In cotton textiles Chinese concerns tended to overinvest in fixed assets in relation to their equity capital, often to the point where all working capital requirements had to be obtained from the market. Not only were many Chinese concerns in a position of over-capacity in relation to equity capital (rather than being under-capitalised) but they were of a size which emphasised their managerial weaknesses [97: 142–155].

The fragmentary evidence available suggests that profits in Chinese manufacturing industry were as high as, and perhaps higher than, those earned in Western (if not Japanese) concerns. In cotton spinning the potential for profits was created by the wide margin between cotton and yarn prices. This remained between 26 and 33 per cent from 1928 to 1933 but fell to only 15 per cent by 1936. However, dividend payments frequently took a guaranteed first call on earnings and deprived companies of funds for reinvestment. There was also a tendency towards speculation in stocks in particular and 'short-termism' in general and Chinese industry registered lower capacity utilisation rates than foreign-owned competitors. Some were overwhelmed by their own managerial difficulties or the exactions of the nationalist government. However, taken as a whole, Chinese enterprises, by adopting new technology, by concentrating on the lower end of the market and by paying lower wages were able to establish and hold a comparative advantage and generated an increasing proportion of total output in the face of competition from both foreign producers and the domestic handicraft sector [97].

The private sector was slow to embrace Western forms of corporate organisation. Although the legislative vacuum had been overcome by the Company Law (*Gongsili*) of 1904 the response to the few corporations which registered was weak and the corporation remained a rarity even in the expansion of the 'golden age'. The values and forms of organisation remained traditional – rooted in family and lineage networks and extending through regional ties, with a reluctance to divorce investment from management. In 1931 only 17.5 per cent of industrial enterprises in Shanghai had adopted a corporate form and 99 per cent of private businesses were still under individual or limited-liability ownership in 1949. A modern sector was emerging but through 'capitalism with Chinese characteristics' [95: 5–7; 100: 48–56].

Moreover, there is now a growing recognition that a range of traditional values, attitudes, institutions and practices which were once regarded as inimical to modernisation were not only capable of adaption and change but provided the bridge across which modernisation could be reached. They may have delayed the onset of modernisation but by the early twentieth century many of the necessary adjustments were being made and the limitations inherent in traditional forms of business organisation, finance, contract and labour management were gradually being overcome [7: 28–53; 95]. Most small and medium-sized Chinese business concerns continued to employ traditional rather than modern accounting systems, for example, but some larger firms adopted double-entry debit–credit conventions, substituted Arabic numerals and abandoned the secrecy which precluded external auditing, whilst others combined Western accounting practices with traditional ethics in order to maintain 'a Confucian culture of collective loyalty and self abnegation' [99: 333–4]. The heritage of traditional Chinese business administration was being built on and provided a context within which Western practices such as cost accounting, quality control and personnel management could be accommodated and moulded to the requirements of the changing Chinese business environment.

Although the Sino-Japanese War (1937–45) was to change the pattern of ownership and disrupt production it could not negate the advances that had been made. By the late 1930s a substantial modern industrial sector had been created and it was one which encompassed both producer and consumer goods and was underpinned not just by modern technology but by a growing assimilation of modern business practices. During the war much more of the Chinese private industrial sector passed into the hands of the state and so, too, did the Japanese assets in China. Even if part of the Manchurian productive capacity was lost as a result of the brief Soviet occupation, the reconstruction of the industrial sector after 1949 and the subsequent expansion during the First Five-Year Plan in the 1950s rested heavily on existing capacity and expertise [102].

6
Agriculture

The symbiosis between constancy and change which underlies the Chinese experience as a whole is nowhere more apparent than in the agricultural sector. Over the two centuries down to 1949, the absence of fundamental change in farming technology and organisation, in the structure of ownership or in the traditional institutions and belief systems imparted a strong element of continuity to the form and rhythm of rural life. The ever-present vulnerability to the vagaries of the climate and the persistent threat of natural or man-made disaster simply served to reinforce the utopian attractiveness of certainty and stability achieved through tried and tested means. At the same time a momentum for change was being generated by a rise in population which outstripped the extension of cultivated area, by the intensified commercialisation which became evident in the second half of the period and by the general breakdown in state–peasant relations which culminated in the intrusion of revolutionary ideals and practices. Progressively, stability could no longer be achieved without change.

From a long-term perspective (i.e. twelfth century onwards) output continued to rise in line with population. Prior to the eighteenth century, output growth resulted from a combination of the extension of cultivated land and productivity gains (Perkins assigns 55 per cent and 45 per cent respectively) [82: 26]. By the early nineteenth century, very little further increase of the cultivated area was possible except in Manchuria and the northwest and the burden of feeding the rising population at existing levels of sustenance fell, almost entirely, on the ability to achieve a commensurate increase in productivity. How then, in the absence of fundamental technological or organisational change, was the necessary productivity advance achieved? In particular, was it possible to raise the productivity of labour sufficiently to enable farmers to advance from their subsistence-level incomes or could those incomes only be protected by the increasing labour supply applying itself to the land at falling rates of marginal productivity?

Before these issues can be tackled it is necessary to establish some basic features of the agrarian economy. In essence, Chinese farming remained village and family-based and was firmly centred on a free peasantry. Over 90 per cent of land was privately owned and worked by owner-occupiers or tenants. Even in the 1930s it seems unlikely that more than 10 per cent of the land was farmed managerially using hired labour – though many farmers, perhaps the majority, relied on seasonal hired labour [68: 290–3; 76: 81]. Elements of 'feudal' subservience and exploitation remained but there was a long-established legal (if not economic or social) equality between landlords and tenants. Resident landlordism dominated in the north while absentee landlordism was gaining ground in the south with much of the land managed through bursaries. Rates of return on land-holding were low and inhibited investment. In the twentieth century returns seldom exceeded 8 per cent before the payment of taxes – well below what could be earned by alternative investment in commerce or money lending [68: 333; 3: 76].

Farming was essentially small-scale and, with partible inheritance, progressively so [81: 243–5]. Most (80 per cent) of the increase to the cultivated area after 1800 lay outside China Proper. Many peasants possessed neither the financial nor the technological capacity to reclaim further waste or marginal land. Reclamation companies offered some relief but probably did no more than compensate for the loss of agricultural land to urban or industrial use and land which became uncultivatable in the wake of natural disaster. Although some very large estates survived, they were few and far between. By the 1930s, the average farm size in China was little more than 24 mu (4 acres) and lower still in the south [68: 268–9]. Farms were unconsolidated, averaging 5.6 parcels across the village. In areas which were terraced – and perhaps as much as one-quarter of the cultivated area was terraced by the 1930s – the plots were often minute [3: 64–5]. Highly intensive farming was a necessity.

The range and distribution of crops were largely determined by climatic conditions. Rice was the dominant crop in the south, wheat and millet formed the staples in the north. Within this dichotomy, variations in the length of the growing season and in the level and regularity of rainfall determined the precise combination of crops including, in the area between the Yangzi and Huai rivers, rice and wheat together (see map 3). Double cropping (not always of rice) was standard in the south; two crops in three years were increasingly prevalent in the north [68; 69; 76]. In addition, farmers grew a myriad of vegetables and an increasing range of industrial crops but, apart from the grasslands on the northern fringes, animals were kept for draught purposes rather than for meat or milk. The high density of population ensured that livestock farming was not economic. Grain farming provided at least three times the food-energy levels of animals from a given unit of land. The necessarily high yields (by pre-modern standards) were achieved by careful and highly labour-intensive husbandry and the application of very high levels of natural fertiliser.

The variation in farm size evident between north and south was largely a function of differences in productivity. Paddy rice yields were between three and five times those of wheat and millet [82: 267]. A latitudinal division between ownership and tenancy is also evident with owner-occupation dominating in the north and tenancy in the south. For China as a whole in the 1930s, 32 per cent of peasants were full tenants and 42 per cent of the cultivated land was rented with the incidence varying from 2 per cent in some areas in the north to 100 per cent in the south [72: 395]. Rents of 50 per cent or more of the main crop were typical. Share rents still dominated but fixed rents in cash were becoming more common [62: 26–34]. The distribution of ownership was also unequal. Communist claims that 10 per cent of the population (landlords and rich peasants) owned 70 to 80 per cent of the land are not borne out by the evidence but the bottom 90 per cent (middle, poor and landless peasants) probably owned no more than 44 per cent [72: 405]. Although high, the degree of inequality was still lower than, for example, in some early modern European economies [3: 83].

It was these differences in land ownership which provided the basis for the exploitation which was the central criterion in the

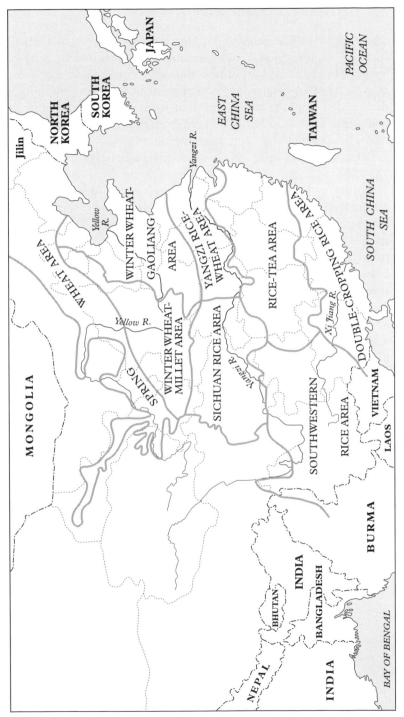

Map 3. China: agricultural regions. Source: [68: 27].

classification of the peasantry adopted by the Communist Party. In brief, landlords and rich peasants owned sufficient land to enable them to exploit others through renting land or hiring labour, middle peasants owned sufficient to avoid exploitation or the need to exploit, whilst the poor owned insufficient to avoid being exploited. Landlords differed from rich peasants in that the whole of their income came from exploitation whilst rich peasants undertook some agricultural work for themselves [54: vol. I, 137–40].

By the early nineteenth century there was already a strong element of commercialisation within the agricultural sector and a significant proportion of output was marketed. Rent income received in kind was marketed by landlords, owner-occupiers placed goods on the market to meet land-tax demands and all peasants traded sufficient of their produce to acquire daily necessities, cover family expenses and pay taxes. Farmers in some areas were already specialising in cotton, opium, tobacco, sugar or mulberry cultivation–silkworm raising. Most trade took place within or between local market centres and the honeycomb of marketing areas and the activities of merchanting intermediaries facilitated a certain amount of long-distance trade, particularly down the great waterways [31]. Lee and Campbell have demonstrated that household structure in the northeastern province of Liaoning changed during the century as families devised new strategies to counter population pressure. 'Diagonal families' where cousins and uncles were coresident with family heads increased disproportionately and it is possible that links will be found between these strategic decisions and the growing commercialisation of family activities [170: 121].

Progressively, if slowly, from the middle of the nineteenth century the development of export markets, the more rapid growth of urban population and the growth of industry (both traditional and modern) combined to generate an increased demand for marketed food grains and agricultural raw materials. Steamships and then the railways improved the long-distance transportation of grain while merchant communities were increasingly able to draw on the services of a developing modern financial sector [81: 250–4].

Liu Ts'ui-jung's study of the upper Han river basin in Southern

Shaanxi provides an example. Stimulated by rising prices peasants, even in the remoter districts, were devoting efforts to generating cash incomes through the market. Exports ranged across broad beans, soy beans, sesame seeds, tobacco leaf, wood oil and various forms of fungus. Shipments of turmeric, an ingredient of tobacco and incense preparation and a speciality of the district, had come to dominate a nationwide market. In the early twentieth century about 700 tons each year were shipped downriver to Hankou (Wuhan) on the Yangzi or transported overland to the northern provinces of Henan, Hebei, Shandong and Gansu yielding 20 million cash [48: 33–4: 69–71].

By the 1930s the proportion of output marketed may have reached 40 per cent (including Manchuria) and in some of the more highly commercialised areas (the lower Yangzi provinces) may have approached 50 per cent [67; 73; 82; 112]. Commercialisation led to diversification for some farmers and specialisation for others and this, in turn, reinforced the process. Farmers who specialised to the point where they were no longer able to supply their own food requirements or who were forced to sell their own high-quality grains turned to their local markets for 'inferior' foodstuffs such as sweet potatoes, thereby widening the scope for commoditisation. In the late nineteenth and early twentieth centuries these developments were encouraged by rising prices and improving terms of trade.

In addition, the pursuit of non-farming activities (textile production, basket weaving, paper making, straw-shoe making, etc.) within the household was a long standing feature of the rural economy (see chapter 2). The expansion of cash-crop output and the processing of those crops for the market rather than for family consumption were mutually dependent and reinforcing. For an increasing proportion of families the deployment of labour in handicraft and other subsidiary pursuits became an integral and vital feature of family income generation rather than a mere supplement to earnings from farming.

Whilst it is possible to detect all of these features it is also necessary to emphasise the degree of variation within the agricultural economy. Rates of population growth, climatic vulnerability, ownership patterns, tenancy rates, social institutions, military disruption, access to transportation and impingement of international trade could all differ so greatly across and within regional, provincial and county boundaries that it is difficult (and often inappropriate) to attempt to generalise about rural conditions across China as a whole. This qualification needs to be borne in mind when the main issues concerning the process and outcome of change are addressed.

Rising population and intensified commercialisation acted as the twin dynamics for change. Population pressure provided the need for change and the labour resources with which to achieve it; commercialisation brought the opportunity and, for many, the incentive. The greater the population pressure the greater the need for commercialisation. But, paradoxically, the greater the degree of commercialisation the greater the extent to which population increase could be accommodated, and the more abundant the supply of labour became the more the need for fundamental change was obviated.

The Taiping and Nian Rebellions were, in part, responses to a population pressure that was, by the mid nineteenth century, almost as extreme as it was to become again in the 1930s. The devastation that accompanied the rebellions was also to be the means by which that pressure was temporarily lightened. By the 1850s, on Perkins' estimates, the average per capita cultivated land availability had fallen to 2.8 mu (assuming that the cultivated area was the same in 1851 as it was in 1873). By 1873 it had risen to 3.5 mu, only to fall back again to 2.9 mu (less than half an acre) by 1933. In four of the five East-Central provinces (Hubei, Jiangxi, Anhui and Zhejiang) most affected by Taiping activities population levels had not regained their mid nineteenth century peak even by 1933 and in the fifth (Jiangsu) it was reached only because of the growth of Shanghai and Nanjing. For these provinces taken as a whole the average per capita land availability rose from 1.8 mu in 1851 to 3.2 mu in 1873 before declining to 2.5 mu – still almost 40 per cent higher than in 1851. Other areas witnessed a much greater deterioration in average farm size from the 1870s – often by more than 30 per cent [82: 212, 236].

Estimates of the amount of land required to reach family subsistence vary considerably and are fraught with danger and misconception. For Hebei and Shandong provinces in the winter wheat–gaoliang (millet) crop area, estimates range from 15 mu [75: 185] to 25 mu [79: 139]. Unfortunately neither source provides any provenance for the figures and neither elucidates on the range of expenses covered by subsistence. The implied daily calorie intake is obviously crucial. Assuming average yields of 150 jin per mu [82: 267] and allowing three crops in every two-year rotation period, a 15 mu (2.5 acre farm) would have yielded 3,375 jin and provided for a daily per capita intake of 3,273 calories (4,676 per male equivalent). As long as no more than 40 per cent of total crop income was required for other outlays – housing, clothing, family expenses, farming expenses (seed grain, fertilisers, etc.), taxes, rents and so on – the residual grain would have provided sustenance at more than 2,000 calories per day. As a result, owner-occupier farms of this size might just have provided for minimal household subsistence expenses though with little, if any, surplus. Families with smaller farms, those which rented land or those unable to achieve average yields would not.

The evidence for the 1930s suggests that the majority of peasants fell into this latter category. Whilst Buck found that the average farm size in the area was 34 mu, 60 per cent of the farms were no more than 20 mu and 26 per cent were less than 10 mu [68: 271]. Moreover, according to Huang almost half of the farms in Hebei and Shandong were smaller than 10 mu [75: 187]. If rent payments are taken into account (and 10 per cent of all households were full tenants and at least another 15 per cent part tenants in the area) [72] it seems possible that the majority of peasant families operated farms which were incapable of giving basic food subsistence from traditional grain farming pursuits alone. General inadequacies are also revealed by Ash's study of Jiangsu and by data collected by the Communist Party for taxation purposes after land reform [62; 83; 84]. According to the latter, two-thirds of all farmers obtained maincrop earnings equivalent to less than 600 jin per capita (2,500 calories per day).

Yet, without seeking to deny or minimise the existence of severe and widespread poverty, it should be remembered that the Buck survey shows an average daily intake per male equivalent of 3,295 calories [68: 407] and other investigations reveal areas where on average families produced well in excess of subsistence or where a proportion of families were able to do so [74: 163, 298–9; 83].

Moreover, on Perkins' figures, output (in the long term) did keep pace with population growth. Riskin has identified a substantial surplus over subsistence [92: 70], Eastman has argued forcefully that the signs of a general tendency towards extreme immiseration prior to 1931 are hard to detect [3: 99–100] and Rawski's claim that output increased more rapidly than population in the period 1914/18 to 1931/6 may have some substance [92].

In aggregate terms output can continue to rise with population as long as average per capita output does not fall. In China, because the farm population constituted a declining proportion of the total and because industrial cash crops were occupying an increasing proportion of the cultivated area, the per capita output of food grains needed to rise. Moreover, further compensatory productivity increases were required in order to offset any efficiency losses emanating from the reduction in farm size. Rising, rather than constant, output per capita was required in order for China to continue to feed her population, supply the additional raw material requirements and prevent the decreasing farm size from pushing a large number of families below subsistence. With average crop yields already at or close to their pre-modern limits the pursuit of productivity gain lay with an increased intensity of crop rotation, the substitution of high-yield and high-value crops (both grain and industrial) and specialisation.

All of these options were labour intensive. The higher-yielding crops required more labour to plant, weed and harvest and some required more irrigation and time spent on the collection, treatment and application of animal, human or vegetable waste as fertiliser. Similarly the unmechanised handicraft activities which offered additional means of raising family output had a high labour input. Because family size had decreased much less rapidly than farm size (even on the smaller farms) the labour–land ratio had risen and the necessary labour resources were available. Farming families needed to devise new strategies for adapting their crop portfolios and for the allocating of their abundant labour between on and off-farm activities. The higher risks and higher input costs of the new crops had to be offset against the potential income gain. The relative merits of employment of family labour on the farm, as hired labour, in handicraft pursuits and in local subsidiary activities needed to be given more careful consideration, as did the possibility of remittance earnings from sons or daughters working away from the village.

Two very different interpretations concerning the nature and outcome of the relationship between population growth and commercialisation have been advanced and they are lines which are often regarded as mutually exclusive. Doubts have been expressed about the validity of the respective assumptions which underlie the two approaches and their findings have been questioned on empirical grounds. Neither viewpoint in itself is entirely convincing as a categorical generalisation. Both are needed in order to encompass the variety and complexity of the agrarian experience.

The more optimistic position has been developed by Brandt, Rawski and Myers [12; 66; 67; 81; 92; 164; 165]. Brandt lays out the case for open, expanding and almost perfectly competitive markets in which households sought to maximise their income and in which 'factors of production were remunerated at levels equal to or near their marginal products'. Real wages and productivity are seen as highly correlated, permitting inferences to be made about productivity trends from real wage data. According to Brandt the evidence points to a rise of 60 to 70 per cent in real wages over the period from the 1870s to the 1930s. The specialisation and competition which more commercialised market operations encouraged raised the marginal productivity of hired labour and, because households allocated labour amongst alternative activities to equalise marginal productivities, the efficiency of family labour must have risen in line with that of hired labour. It was this rise in productivity which allowed average per capita incomes to rise. Moreover, poor families, by increasing their labour input in handicraft and subsidiary occupations more rapidly, were able to narrow their income differential with the rich [67].

The assumptions and the representativeness of data which lie behind these conclusions have both been questioned and Brandt's later work demonstrates a more acute awareness of agricultural nuances and complexities [89: 295–307]. Faure is surely right to argue that whilst markets were not monopolistic nor were they unfettered [73: 97] and the price correlations which Brandt takes as evidence of the operation of competitive markets are seen by others as indicative of oligopolist market arrangements [166; 167; 168].

Credence must also be given to Hamilton's contention that the dominant influence on market stability was 'clannishness' rather than the natural laws of supply and demand [8: 84]. Labour and loan markets were not always as open and competitive as Brandt assumes and the estimates of the level to which real wages had risen seem excessively high. Taking payments in kind together with the cash wage, Brandt suggests an annual income of 20 to 25 piculs of grain for hired labourers – sufficient to provide 2,000 calories per day for each member of a family of five. Other evidence points to earnings being inadequate to support a family leaving wage labour as the recourse, and fate, of the single male [75: 199]. More fundamentally, much more evidence is necessary to demonstrate that peasants were motivated by considerations of profit or income maximisation or attempted to equate marginal productivities.

Huang [75; 76; 161; 162] argues a rather different and less optimistic stance, taking issue with both the reality of perfectly competitive markets and the supposed neo-classical assumption that commercialisation and specialisation necessarily lead to increases in labour productivity (at least in the sense of output per work day). For Huang, peasants became involved in commercialised production more because they were extraction driven (by landlords) or survival driven than because they were enterprise driven. The rationality of survival was the dominant motivation not profit maximisation. Huang's conceptual framework is drawn from Chayanov rather than Adam Smith and rests on two main propositions: that peasants do not perceive activities in terms of marginal returns and that they employ family labour until subsistence needs are met, even if the rate of return falls 'irrationally' below the market rate or fails to cover subsistence costs. In less than perfect market conditions Chinese peasants sought security through the commoditisation of production, diversification and/or specialisation and by increasing the number of days worked on both farming and handicraft activities. This more intensive use of family labour – what Huang terms the 'familisation of production' – enabled farmers to raise output and increase per capita output, but only at the expense of diminished returns to scale. Thus, commercialisation and output growth were not accompanied by development (defined as increased returns per work day); a combination that Huang designates as 'involution'.

Involution was not new (it can be traced back to Ming times) and it was to continue into the post-1949 era under the guise of co-operative farming, but it was given powerful momentum by the population pressure and intensified commercialisation of the nineteenth and early twentieth centuries. Urban and industrial development came to be interlocked with rural involution. A symbiotic relationship developed between a flourishing urban industrial sector and peasant production. Urban industry (and export markets) provided the demand which underwrote the labour-surplus involuted commercialisation of both grain and non-grain peasant production, and provided the main raw material (machine yarn) which facilitated the familisation of peasant farming.

As a result, commercialisation and the attendant familisation of production did not normally lead to an improvement in welfare and did not generate transformative growth. In households which were able to increase the number of labour days sufficiently to offset the diminished marginal returns, household income could increase. In others which were not, income fell. At best, the more intensive use of labour, often at sub-subsistence rates of return, brought survival in the face of population pressure; at worst, the higher risks involved in a greater dependence on the market forced small family farmers down into tenancy or out onto the labour market.

According to Huang most factor markets for short-term labour, animal power and fertilisers on the North China Plain were sufficiently open for poor peasants, on average, to achieve the same yield per unit of land as middle peasants and as their larger managerial counterparts. Small farmers, however, were not able to use their increased labour inputs as efficiently and achieved a much lower total factor productivity (if labour inputs are costed at the going wage rate). It was the ability, and willingness, to tolerate less than subsistence returns to labour that helped household cotton-textile producers to hold out against mechanised competition. Income differentials were not narrowed. If anything, polarisation was taking place in the countryside. Independent farmers were being forced onto the labour market (proletarianisation) at the bottom and larger managerial farms were moving up to rentier landlordism at the top.

Whilst the majority of historians still seem to find the Brandt/

Rawski methodology and precise quantification of output growth
and productivity change unconvincing, neither has Huang's analysis found universal acceptance. Critics have pointed to Huang's
misrepresentation of the Smithian position as demanding an
inevitable causal relationship between commercialisation, specialisation and gains in the marginal productivity of labour, and doubt
whether categorical general conclusions can be drawn from what
is still a severely limited data base. Yet Huang's analysis may well
come closer to encapsulating the experience of large numbers of
peasant farmers – perhaps the majority – than Brandt's and, if the
kind of rigidities which once characterised the debate between
'pessimists' and 'optimists' or 'distributionists' and 'technologists'
can be eased away, it is possible that the two views can be
contained within a spectrum of rural experience.

It is important to recognise the diversity of motivation and
experience prevalent within the rural economy. Most households
attempted to maximise income in order to survive, improve their
standard of living and ensure an adequate inheritance for their
children – though some were content to opt for a high leisure
preference once subsistence had been assured [74]. It is no more
reasonable to argue that all peasants operated in perfectly competitive markets, were driven by motives of profit maximisation, were
able to raise their productivity and experience real income gains
than to suppose that all peasants were locked into a subsistence
ethic and could do no more than protect incomes at the expense of
falling marginal rates of return.

Definitive verdicts on the process and outcome of agricultural
change across the period must await the availability of more
detailed, direct and comprehensive evidence, both spatially and
across time, concerning output, rates of labour usage, marginal
productivity and subsistence levels. Nevertheless, at the risk of
over-simplification certain tentative conclusions can be drawn.

There is a consensus that output continued to rise in line with a
population that increased by more than two-thirds to exceed
500 million, that average incomes did not fall and that there was a
long-term increase in the productivity of the land. All this was in
the absence of a technological transformation. The traditional
advanced organic economy had displayed a remarkable capacity
for expansion and change.

The explanation for these output and productivity gains derives largely from the intensified commercialisation that increasingly characterised the rural economy. Rising population, increasing demand (from the modern urban sector and exports) and the struggle to protect or enhance living standards in the face of falling average farm size and the exactions of the 'feudal' landlord system were the dynamics. Households adopted more intensive crop cycles, substituted high for low-yielding grain crops, switched from grain to non-grain crops, hired out labour, allocated more labour to handicraft pursuits and became more heavily involved in market transactions. Agricultural and rural commercialisation – encompassing intensification, specialisation, diversification and familisation – was the means by which some families were able to prosper and the majority to survive. It enabled some households – tenants and owner-occupiers alike – to raise their productivity sufficiently to offset the reduction in farm size, whilst others increased the intensity of their labour input in their attempt to compensate for that reduction. The net effect was increased output, improved unit-land yields and a changed structure of output, but not necessarily higher average per capita incomes [75; 76; 161; 162].

This analysis, emphasising the diversity of motivation and experience, has implications for the growth and development debate at the aggregate level. The more the market departed from conditions of perfect competition and the greater the diversity of peasant motivations the less convincing the Brandt/Rawski case for generalised labour-productivity gains becomes, the more tenuous the argument that output growth exceeded population and the more equivocal it is necessary to be about the onset of modern economic growth. The possibility cannot be ruled out, but the case is weakened.

This, in turn, has a bearing on the question of whether the capacity for real income growth in the rural economy had been exhausted. The closer that boundary was approached, the stronger the case for fundamental change. It is clear that the agrarian economy was in a state of crisis in the 1930s. Short-term factors – exceptionally unfavourable climatic conditions, political and military instability, increased state exactions, the collapse of crucial export markets, etc. – combined with the longer-term effects of population pressure on farm size to devastating effect. And handicrafts were coming under much more severe pressure from Chinese producers in the modern sector.

If the problems were exclusively of a short-term nature and if Rawski is right that in free market conditions profit-maximising peasants would inevitably find ways of raising productivity, then the return of stability and the creation of open markets should, in themselves, ensure efficiency gains. But if farm size had been reduced to the point where it was no longer possible for the majority to generate subsistence incomes additional measures were necessary. There is sufficient evidence to suggest that, within the limits imposed by pre-modern technology and the existing socio-economic framework, this position was being approached. Whereas in 1800 the majority of farming families might have been able to meet subsistence requirements from traditional grain farming alone, by the middle of the twentieth century they could not.

The reduction in farm size meant that for a sizeable minority, perhaps even the majority, the commercialisation of crop production and the greater integration of handicraft activities had become essential for survival. General immiseration may have been avoided but indebtedness was rising and many families were forced to reduce their food intake alarmingly. It may be an exceptional case but David and Isabel Crook found families surviving on 10 oz. of grain a day – less than 1,000 calories [70: 120]. Without societal and technological change the further liberalisation of markets might only have provided further involution, with peasants responding by increasing inputs of labour at declining marginal rates of productivity [76].

From the perspective of the 1990s it would seem to be the re-opening of markets together with the promotion of small-scale rural industrialisation within a society organised very differently from that of the past which eventually transformed productivity and incomes in the countryside. It was precisely this solution – rural industrialisation in a market context – which Fei Xiaotong, amongst others, was beginning to advocate in the 1940s [74]. In the meantime collectivism was the chosen alternative, though whatever the advances it brought in enabling foodgrain output to keep pace with population it did not prove capable of achieving the necessary diversification, specialisation or increase in labour productivity to allow real incomes to rise. Chinese agriculture and, indeed, the rural economy as a whole continued on an involutionary path for another quarter of a century.

7

The state and the economy

The traditional function of the state was to provide and ensure economic stability and it was a function which was fulfilled successfully during the early Qing expansion of the eighteenth century. By the end of the next century the same role was no longer tenable. Internationally, governments were accepting, or were being forced to accept, the responsibility not for maintaining economic equilibrium but for the promotion of change through industrialisation. It was a role which the Qing government was reluctant to accept and, according to Feuerwerker, one that it was incapable of playing since its 'ideology, traditional fiscal practices, and patterns of behaviour were all obstacles to suitable action' [43: 59]. In this view the backward-looking, exploitative and corrupt practices of the state constituted the major barriers to rational economic development [25: 1; 144; 153]. The government neither took the promotional role itself nor did it create the context within which private entrepreneurs were able to respond effectively and this deficiency clearly contributed to China's slow progress towards modernisation.

Yet, as our understanding of the activities of the Qing state has deepened it has become clear that any simple characterisation of the state as the rigid defender of conservatism opposing all change on principle is misleading. Studies of the early Qing have demonstrated that the state was capable of generating patterns of behaviour and institutions which were by no means inimical to economic expansion and change. And once the actions of the state are seen in terms of its own aims – 'social stability, internal security, and strategic-logistical control of the empire' – a rather different picture begins to emerge [25: 1]. In the nineteenth century when new, more difficult challenges emerged, the ability to address old internal problems diminished and the reality fell further short of the ideal. But bridges between tradition and modernity were being built. Leading figures in the provincial bureaucracy, and a few in the government itself, were seeking, and taking, steps towards industrialisation. Even if industrialisation was not yet seen as an end in itself it had, by the end of the century, come to be seen as a means towards the end of national survival and strength.

In order to develop an analysis of the Chinese state's struggle with mounting domestic economic problems and the encroachment of Western power in the nineteenth century it is necessary to establish a number of the fundamental elements of Qing political economy; a political economy that was different from its European counterpart but which, within its own terms of reference, proved remarkably successful.

The Confucian political economy to which the state adhered was that of an agrarian empire and was directed above all to the maintenance of social stability through the guarantee of minimal standards of survival and the amelioration of unacceptable inequalities. As Wong puts it 'the ideal Chinese political economy was an agrarian commercial economy in which expansion came from opening new lands and improving productivity on already cultivated fields' and where rural industry would complement cash crops to balance supply and demand through rural exchange [15: 138]. But as a consequence, although commercial expansion could be (and was) actively supported, the institutions and practices which helped to create commercial capitalism in Europe did not evolve because they were deemed unnecessary or inappropriate. The state did not view commerce as an important source of revenue (either through taxation or merchant loans) and no strong dynamic symbiotic relationship with a wealthy profit-seeking merchant community developed. Moreover, an ethic in which the superior man was guided by the quest for benevolence, righteousness and frugality sat uneasily with the glorification (or even the official tolerance) of the unbridled pursuit of profit for its own sake, the rise of conspicuous consumption and concentrations of mercantile wealth.

Nor, whilst promoting expanded production, could the system

easily accept the rise of urban industrialisation for it would not benefit the agrarian society as a whole and, through the creation of regional disparities and possible class differences, appeared neither reasonable or desirable. Similarly, the high priority accorded to equality and mutual benefit made it difficult to even imagine aggressive mercantilist or competitive free-trade policies designed to promote wealth and power at the expense of other states [15: 136–50]. In short, whilst China's political economy possessed strengths in its own right and was pursued successfully throughout the eighteenth century the inherent limitations were revealed in the new nineteenth-century international context. The depth of the commitment to the entrenched political economy ensured that the adjustment was a protracted and painful one.

Although it has been argued that the commercialised agrarian expansion of the eighteenth century was largely a 'private sector phenomenon untouched by the hand of the state' [12; 152: 503] it is now recognised that the state played an important role, albeit at one remove. With the Finance Ministry (*Hubu*) acting as its key agent [148: 9] the Qing state accepted a general responsibility for the people's livelihood, encouraged agricultural expansion, promoted the development of a commercial handicraft production system, regularised the land tax, reorganised and maintained the granary system and controlled the money supply. In doing so it took over some of the responsibilities of the gentry and manipulated the local elites in support of its initiatives [152: 503–4]. And, whilst production and commerce became increasingly privatised, the state's interaction with those private interests was pursued within the traditional concept of 'administrative brokerage' [3: 130–3]. Licensed agents acted as brokers between the government and the public in order to facilitate the increase in trade, protect the public and serve the state. In some cases they operated within the context of a tight monopoly (salt, copper, ginseng, the Imperial textile and porcelain manufactories), whilst in the management of local administrative tasks (water conservancy, granaries, tax collection) the arrangements were based on the principle of guarantorship [25: 5].

Whilst the result was a mixture of support, neglect and extraction [3: 130], the extent of the state's intervention in the economy was considerable. The granary system was capable of feeding

5 per cent of the provincial populations for 15 per cent of the year and could have handled as much as 7 per cent of marketed grain. Moreover, with the outlay running at between 0.5 and 1.25 million taels per year on average, the cost may have been as high as 2 per cent of total state revenue and 5 per cent or more of non-military expenditure. The Qing state's willingness and capacity to underwrite the people's livelihood at this level for over a century may well have been unmatched in the early modern world and, in comparison with previous dynasties, 'served the needs of a greater variety of people, over a broader area, and for a longer time' [152: 493–8].

But if the state's approach contained a number of strengths and offered positive precedents for the future it also exhibited weaknesses and these were to have important consequences for the government's ability to influence or control the economy in the nineteenth century. In a general sense the ideal political economy was conceived as an agrarian economy in which the state sought to soften inequalities and guarantee subsistence. Concentrations of wealth arising from private market manipulation which commercial and, to an even greater extent, industrial capitalism would bring were regarded with suspicion, if not hostility. Although Chinese political economy rested on well-developed markets, it lacked the financial and business institutions which were developing in Europe and the continued commitment to a particular agrarian political economy perspective inevitably conditioned the response [15: 138–9, 150–1].

Within this context two particular problems were evident. The first was the lack of effective financial leverage. Taxes on commerce were generally low and the land tax, which provided 80 per cent of income prior to the 1850s, was fixed. Increased revenue was highly dependent on new land being brought into cultivation and registered. Even with new taxes – the *lijin* (transit) and the Maritime Customs – the government took only between 6 and 7 per cent of GDP, and in times of rising prices rather less. Central government in Beijing received no more than 3 per cent [43]. This deficiency prompted the initiation of arbitrary (and often corrupt) exactions and, in the absence of private institutions capable of mobilising funds on a large scale, left the economy more vulnerable to the influence of foreign capital and investment [7: 27; 95: 17].

Secondly, the effectiveness of that leverage was highly dependent on the quality of the service provided by the administration –
the mandarinate and its gentry and merchant agents. The prin-
cipal virtues of the Confucian scholar-official were his (women
were not eligible for the examinations, even if educated) moral
uprightness and frugality. The more commercialised expansion of
the eighteenth century had brought new opportunities for financial
gain (if not corruption) and the standard of the service provided
by the officials and their gentry assistants had declined – though
not to the extent that was once thought [38]. However, even if
Confucian propriety was fully restored most officials lacked the
willingness, experience or know-how to foster and manage economic modernisation. Whilst industrial modernisation was considered too important to be left to private entrepreneurs it is
doubtful whether an effective merchant-official response could
have been generated exclusively within the confines of the
brokerage system.

By the early nineteenth century the economy had become much
more vulnerable. The severity and combination of the problems
was novel and the Qing leadership's assumption that economic
disorder bred political discord ensured that the situation would be
taken seriously. The reaction to the grain shipment crisis of the
1820s is an indication of the ability to mobilise resources on a
large scale in an attempt to secure the interests of the state without
disrupting the people's livelihood [141]. But the response, in its
general conception, was still to draw heavily on tradition and was
to centre on the notion of a 'Restoration'.

Although frequently analysed narrowly in terms of the Tong Zhi
reign (1861–74) the process, as Pong has argued, is more effectively viewed as a general Qing Restoration reaching back to the
Opium War and extending on into the 1880s [28]. Its generation
lay with the advocates of 'Practical Stagecraft' who diagnosed
internal dynastic decline and showed a willingness to question
traditional but ineffective institutions. In the 1840s a few reform-
minded officials recognised the additional threat posed by the
West and sought means to counter the internal problems and
contain the external influence. China was to strengthen herself by
returning to the pursuit of traditional Confucian virtues and
defend herself against the West by absorbing military technology

from the West. During the Tong Zhi period these ideas were promoted at the centre by Prince Gong (Kung) and made explicit in the *ziqiang* (self-strengthening) and *yangwu* (foreign affairs) movements [47; 131; 133; 146]. For governor-general Li Hongzhang (Li Hung-chang) these principles also required the pursuit of economic sovereignty (*lichuan*) [133: 8–9].

The Restoration succeeded in delaying dynastic collapse but it did not lead to the military and economic modernisation necessary to preclude the West and save the dynasty. A start was made – arsenals, mines, steamship lines and a telegraph service were established, and new sources of revenue were introduced – but it did not amount to a modernisation programme. In the 1880s the reformist ideas which the restorationist movement had spawned were curtailed temporarily when Confucian fundamentalism reasserted itself, though the ideas and the reaction against them in turn gave rise to the more sweeping structural and institutional changes of the Reform Movement in the 1890s.

The court needed to work closely with both provincial leaders and local elites and merchant communities, and to make sufficient finance available to initiate and sustain the modernisation measures. In the event an uneasy tension developed between the provinces and the centre, and initiatives by leading officials such as Li Hongzhang and Zhang Zhidong (Chang Chih-tung) were not supported strongly enough by the centre to become generalised. The problem was partly one of finance. The centre could not raise sufficient funds to maintain traditional services, increase military expenditure and underwrite widespread modernisation. Whilst the modernising officials were not allocated the necessary guaranteed financial support, the funds that they did receive deprived inland areas which were suffering as a result of a reorientation of trade towards the coast and the breakdown in long-standing employment-generating facilities (such as the Grand Canal) [145].

But even if the finance had been available it is not entirely clear that the centre would have supported a widespread modernisation programme. Although the Restoration was far from being the exclusively conservative phenomenon that it was once made out to be, its underlying ideology did inevitably conflict with the pursuit of fundamental change [146] and whilst some provincial officials (for example Shen Baochen) were both loyal Confucians and advocates of radical change, others used the Restoration to gain greater independence [130: 110].

By the early 1870s a tension had emerged between the need to establish modern enterprises and a reluctance on the part of the merchant community to become involved in their promotion. Merchants were prepared to invest in foreign ventures but not in indigenous enterprises. With the creation of the first joint stock company (*gongsi*) – The China Merchants' Steam Navigation Company – in 1872, Li Hongzhang offered the dual means of overcoming this obstacle and starting the trend towards 'economic sovereignty' [133: 9; 140: 140]. Through the *guandu shangban* (government supervision–merchant management) format Li provided a combination of enterprise autonomy and official political protection and financial patronage, in this case in the form of subsidies and monopoly shipping rights. Merchant investment was forthcoming and for more than a decade the venture succeeded. Li had demonstrated that the state could intervene in a positive way and provide a model which might balance private and public requirements.

After 1885, however, a combination of Li's gradual political decline and the state's worsening financial position undermined the initiative. The state sought to extract from rather than subsidise the company and management was placed in the hands of Sheng Xuanhuai (Sheng Hsuan-huai) [42]. Increasing bureaucratic interference and control led to a fall in profits and a failure to re-invest in new technology and not only induced merchants to withdraw their investment but led to their disenchantment with government-sponsored enterprises and a general reluctance to invest in other modern ventures [140]. The company had become 'ensnared in the conflict between national goals and private gain' [131: 461], though political exigencies rather than the value system or market forces had proved to be the limiting factor.

State supervision had been replaced by bureaucratic control. Private and bureaucratic capitalism now co-existed in an uneasy and unproductive alliance. Most large-scale industry was controlled by the government and was dependent on the state for patronage, capital and protection from excessive squeeze. Private industry was still to grow rapidly (see chapter 5) but Li's vision of a leading role for the state in the promotion of modern industrial ventures lapsed and the opportunity for an effective alliance between industry and the state had been dissipated [133: 11]. Nor had the state yet transformed the nature of scientific enquiry or the role of science within society. A very small minority within the elite had begun to move but the court, or even the leading self-strengtheners, did little to foster scientific research or enhance the position of science within the education system, nor was the need for science to contribute to the process of economic change fully recognised [147: 72–4].

The Sino-Japanese (1894) war revealed the extent to which the military self-strengthening had failed and the relationship between Confucianism and modernisation took on a new dimension. The *ti-yong* idea ('Chinese learning for the essence, Western learning for the application') gave the reassurance of continuity but implied a need for institutional reform. On the economic side a more wide-ranging commitment to modernisation became evident [14: 231]. The Reform Movement of 1898 may have been short-lived but by identifying the need to raise more revenue, develop a national railway network, encourage a machine industry and shipping, exploit indigenous mineral resources, unify and stabilise the currency and establish a national postal system it did set out a programme for China's economic development [13: 39].

The nineteenth century had transformed the context in which the state operated. Its traditional authority and ability to exercise the power required of oriental despotism had been weakened. The strengthening of regionalism in the face of that decline in auto-cratic control was leading inexorably to the emergence of modern warlordism. Also, with the growing intrusion of state power into societal and economic processes, a new tension between local elites and the state was emerging. For further progress towards modernisation to be made in the new century the centre needed to regain political and military authority and devise and implement a strategy for modernisation which would gain the support of local interest groups [150].

The initial practical steps came with the reforms of the final years of the Qing dynasty. These included the promulgation of the first Company Law (*Gongsili*) in 1904, the reform of the examination system, the recognition of commercial and agricultural associations, and culminated in the move towards constitutional change. The *Gongsili* redefined the state's relationship with the business community and marked the recognition of a legitimate independent role for private mercantile initiative [7: 30–1]. By clearing the way for the adoption of corporate forms of business activity, it was explictly designed to promote China's economic development, thought it was also seen as a means by which the case for ending extraterritoriality could be enhanced. Even if, as Kirby has argued, the assumption that the modern Western corporation was the appropriate and necessary model for successful private development has proved mistaken (it was to be the government which was to be the main beneficiary of corporate possibilities), the law did contribute to the eventual restoration of sovereignty [100: 43–4].

The dominant ideology behind the pursuit of economic modernisation in the twentieth century was provided by Sun Zhongshan (Sun Yat-sen). Against the background of 'The Three Principles of the People' (nationalism, democracy and people's livelihood) Sun set out a strategy for China's international development and a means of solving the 'land problem'. Sun admired the achievements of Western democratic capitalism but recognised some of the inherent weaknesses – unemployment, inequality and exploitation. He argued that, as a backward economy, China could learn from the more advanced economies and draw on their resources in order to match and then surpass them. In the aftermath of the First World War the West, because of its own position of severe over-capacity, would have a vested interest in financing the development of China as a market. China would be able to draw in foreign capital to finance a programme which echoed the aborted reform measures of 1898 – the construction of 100,000 miles of railway and a million miles of Macadamised roads, the development of commercial harbours, the creation of modern cities with public utilities, the establishment of large-scale iron and steel and cement works, the modernisation of traditional handicraft industries, etc. [135; 149].

In order to facilitate these developments Sun favoured the creation of a mixed economy. Private enterprise was to be encouraged, protected and regulated but where it was not forthcoming or where monopolies or national interests (and these included heavy industry and communications) were at stake national undertakings would be established. In the agricultural sector Sun advocated the 'equalisation of land rights' and a programme of technical assistance. Land was to be passed to the tiller not through revolutionary confiscation but through taxation. Sun drew on Henry George to argue that unearned rises in land values as industrialisation and urbanisation occurred should be taxed and, in the process, ownership transferred to the tiller [135; 149].

Sun saw the need for a democratic constitutional framework but recognised that substantial preparatory work was needed before a genuinely representative democratic government could be installed. In the interim he suggested a period of 'tutelage' under which an unelected Republican government would educate the people and create the necessary institutions for democracy [137].

Whilst Sun's plans for China's international development were naive, utopian and far too heavily dependent on foreign capital, those for land equalisation impractical and those for the regulation of capital open to corruption, his revolutionary pedigree ensured that they were endorsed by both of the main political parties – Guomindang (Kuomintang) and Communist (CCP). Each sought legitimacy by attempting to put the ideas into effect.

The revolution of 1911 ended imperial rule but did not usher in a strong Republican government. The forces of regionalism ensured that China lapsed into warlordism. The Guomindang and the Communists joined forces in 1924 to launch the Northern Expedition and reclaim China from warlord fragmentation but, alarmed by rising peasant activism and distrustful of Communist ambitions Jiang Jieshi (Chiang Kai-shek) brought the fragile United Front to an end in 1927 once a new power base in Shanghai had been consolidated. After 1928, although the Nationalist government controlled most of the eastern seaboard and the lower Yangzi valley (and, therefore, most of the crucial modern sector), autonomy had to be conceded to warlords across Manchuria and much of northern and western China. Then, in 1931, Manchuria was formally annexed by Japan.

Yet China's 'disintegration' into political instability and regional militarism once identified as the main limiting factor on progress towards modernisation [59] is not now seen in quite the same exclusively negative light. Military action and disruption to lines of transport and communication did adversely affect some areas but no more than 2 per cent of the adult male population was mobilised at any one time, total casualties between 1917 and 1930 amounted to under 400,000, military spending by central government probably never exceeded 2 per cent of total output prior to 1937 and the extraction of resources by provincial and local governments for military purposes remained modest. The scale of military activity before the outbreak of the Sino-Japanese war was simply insufficient to have invoked a general economic or social crisis [92]. Moreover, some industries received a stimulus from military orders; in areas of military stability (such as Shanxi) individual warlord regimes were able to provide 'benefits that partly, and perhaps entirely, offset the negative economic effects of military control' [92: 45]; and the Japanese began to create a heavy industrial base in Manchuria [175; 177; 178].

The pursuit of an enhanced military capacity also brought China into closer economic contact with Germany. By the 1930s the aims of the state had changed. Lip service was still paid to the people's livelihood but the real impetus was now given by the creation of wealth for the state and the regime's industrial self-sufficiency. For ideological, political and economic reasons heavy industry was to be state controlled and for the Guomindang planners the pursuit of an industrial capacity to fight a modern war became paramount. Germany served as a model and Germany was the only nation willing to help on China's terms [138: 255–62].

The overall economic achievement of the Nationalist government and its record of economic management over the 'Nationalist' or 'Nanjing' decade (1928–37) remain contentious issues. In terms of macro-economic management a number of important advances were made. Tariff autonomy was regained and the Customs Gold Unit adopted to safeguard revenue against fluctuating exchange rates, the *lijin* tax was abolished, a new currency (the yuan) was introduced and in 1935 a paper currency adopted, a Central Bank was established in 1928 and a Reserve Bank in 1935, the complex weights and measures system was simplified and modernised, the budget was put on a modern footing and expanded, complex land and labour laws were drafted and promulgated, and a proportion of China's international debt was repaid [156]. All of these measures contributed to the growth of the economy, though their potential benefits were often undermined by the government's inability to follow them through or by conflicts in its own strategy [51].

It is now clear that one of the government's more impressive contributions lay in the field of science. The creation of political stability and the more active promotion of science – even if on largely utilitarian grounds – encouraged China's second generation of scientists to return from abroad. The Nationalists not only put resources into science education but had a hand in all of the scientific developments of the period. An indigenous science-based chemical industry was created and output grew. Yet growth quickly reached the limits set by the size of the Chinese market and the industry could not absorb the increasing number of qualified graduates. Moreover, the conflict between the growth of state power and professional scientific expertise and autonomy was never resolved and probably heightened as the decade wore on [147: 174–6, 202–7, 285–6].

In agriculture, by contrast, the 1930 Land Law which set out statutory rent and interest-rate reductions was never fully put into effect. The government's military preoccupation with the Communist threat deprived it of the necessary financial resources to assist any programme of agricultural improvement and the attempt to impose rent reductions stalled because it threatened to undermine the economic position of its main support base in the countryside, the landlord class. Although Bernhardt has shown that landlord enforcement of high rents was constrained in some areas [65] the effects of increases in local surtaxes more than outweighed any relief to peasant cultivators [51]. The Nationalists may have limited landlord power but they did not challenge it. Yet, by undermining the position of local elites an authority vacuum appeared within village communities in North China which further weakened the economic fabric of the countryside and made the area more susceptible to revolutionary infiltration [75].

Similarly, although the government's relationship with the business community had moved on from that of the nineteenth century, it was still not a mutually supportive association. The relationship remained a complex one with the state neither acting on the behalf of a capitalist class which had greatly strengthened its position after 1911 nor operating exclusively as a rapacious force against it. Whilst the Guomindang sought to promote indigenous import-substituting capitalism, it was constrained by the context in which it operated and had a limited capacity to deliver on the objective. The extent to which the government could mitigate the effects of the international depression in a situation where China was a small player and a price-taker was modest and its actions were further circumscribed by its incomplete regional authority [155].

The business community looked to the government for a lowering of the tax burden, increased tariff protection and financial assistance in its struggle to combat falling prices and profits and a high degree of over-capacity, and it recognised the need for a measure of intervention and control in return. In the event, the government was unwilling and unable to provide the assistance because, although it was predisposed to help, it continued to place political priorities above economic ones. Its overriding concerns were to placate Japan and achieve internal unity by annihilating the Communists. Trade concessions and revenue priorities weighed more heavily than the health of private industry which was regarded by some as managerially incompetent, financially unsound and more a source of wealth than a motor of development [138: 80; 155].

Despite the creation of new bureaucratic mechanisms through which intervention could have been made effective – the National Economic Council under Song Ziwen (T. V. Soong) was the prime example – light industry remained overwhelmingly in private hands before the outbreak of war. State control over the banking sector had been imposed in order to guarantee financial support but, in Wright's view, bureaucratic capital should still be seen as part of capitalist enterprise without necessarily representing a threat to the development of national capital. However, national capital, and the national capitalists, were not able to resist the government's encroachment and in the changed conditions of the war the ideological foundations, the mechanisms and the motivations were there for the ascendancy of bureaucratic capital in light as well as heavy industry [95: 15–16; 134; 155]. By 1943, 70 per cent of the paid-up capital of enterprises in the Nationalist controlled areas was in the hands of the state. And, even if the private sector had not yet embraced corporatism, the government's Five- and Ten-Year Plans reveal a clear vision of a future dominated by corporate state capitalism [100: 53–6].

The government's economic actions certainly did not prevent growth from taking place and, in a number of important ways, contributed to a process of growth that was already under way. Quantitatively, however, central government leverage was little greater than it had been in the nineteenth century. Expenditure remained below 4 per cent of GDP and well over half was directed towards military or debt repayment purposes [92]. In the short term, factors outside government control – the international depression, catastrophic weather conditions, the international price of silver and the Japanese invasion – were all more decisive determinants of the course of economic change. The government neglected agriculture and probably misunderstood the real nature of the agrarian problem. It had distorted the growth of the rising private modern sector and had used Sun's ideas on the regulation of capital to sanction an increase in bureaucratic control for private gain. And, by moving the economy onto a managed currency in 1935, it had paved the way for the hyper-inflation of the 1940s.

In giving priority to political unification and the reimposition of strong central control in order to redress the heightened regionalism which warlordism represented, and in attempting to revive the values of the neo-Confucian restorationist strategy, the Nationalist government maintained clear lines of continuity with the past. By accepting a greater responsibility for China's economic modernisation and by following Sun Zhongshan and adopting a more interventionist approach to modernisation it became even more involved in economic and societal processes. In doing so the old gulf between the government and local elites widened further.

Many of the problems and dilemmas of the nineteenth century remained. The government had accepted a greater responsibility for China's economic modernisation and on balance its 'nation-building' efforts had contributed positively to the creation of a modern economy. But, at the same time, it had done little to enhance or even defend the livelihood of the vast majority of the agrarian population and it had distorted the growth of the urban private sector. Corruption and chronic economic and financial mismanagement in the 1940s were then to undermine, and ultimately destroy, its authority and legitimacy [57; 61; 136].

8
Conclusion: the legacy of the past

In the period under review China can be characterised, in essence, as a land-scarce but labour-abundant agrarian economy confronting the limits of its pre-modern base (both socio-economic and technological) and being drawn into contact with an industrialising West. Whilst there is now a deeper and more satisfying understanding of the complex process of change which that context framed and helped to determine, the precise outcome in terms of the creation of a modern growth economy remains uncertain.

There is no doubt that the period witnessed a considerable expansion of output or that, over time, output growth matched that of population. Nor is there any disagreement that a modern industrial sector was created during the first third of the twentieth century, and on a scale sufficient to underwrite a future socialist industrialisation programme. The incorporation of Western technology, the adjustment of a variety of Chinese business practices and the emergence of new facilitating institutions had enabled the transition to urban, mineral energy-based industrialisation to take hold, at least in certain areas.

However, whilst growth at the aggregate level cannot be ruled out, neither can it be proved. Although the creation of capitalism with Chinese characteristics was well under way it had come too late for modern industry to assume a sufficiently large quantitative role in the economy to compensate for any lack of growth in the dominant agricultural sector prior to 1937. Deficiencies in the range and reliability of the surviving production data preclude (and may always preclude) the elimination of the margin of error obscuring the crucial distinction between growth and non-growth in the agricultural sector by direct means. And despite the ingenious and forceful harnessing of indirect evidence behind the case for growth, so many methodological and empirical doubts remain that the unequivocal identification of sustained advances in average real output and incomes is still not possible and the proposition must remain, at best, a likelihood [89]. As a result, China may be the only major economy for which it is not yet possible to ascertain whether modern economic growth at the aggregate level had taken hold prior to 1950.

As far as the process of change is concerned, the major analytical initiatives in recent years have derived from the application of classical and neo-classical thinking to the Chinese economy. This has brought a deepening of the understanding of the causal mechanisms which underlay the Chinese experience and has led to a reappraisal of some of the Western assumptions relating to the emergence of a modern economic growth path. Rawski and Brandt have argued for a neo-classical openness of product and factor markets, implying the inevitability of productivity gains along European lines. Others have expressed reservations about the degree of openness (particularly in factor markets) whilst Hung has questioned the application of the neo-classical paradigm as a whole and advanced the concept of 'involution' to explain the absence of labour-productivity gains. More recently, R. Bin Wong has argued that the Chinese economy of the eighteenth century with its characteristic proto-industrial component did not generate transformative change from within itself, nor was it subsequently permeated by the institutions of China's own emerging industrial capitalism. Rather, the rural economy continued to function within the confines of the classical economist's world of Smithian dynamics bounded by Malthusian constraints. There is nothing inevitable about the emergence of European-style industrialisation and in this scenario the vast bulk of the Chinese economy continued to operate in the way that Adam Smith had expected and predicted whilst Europe broke away from the constraints [15].

These various approaches are not necessarily incompatible and a persuasive explanation of the dynamics of change almost certainly requires a diversity of approach and a willingness to encompass and integrate a range of conceptual initiatives. The size, diversity and complexity of the economy certainly militate against easy generalisation or simple mono-causal explanation concerning the process of change. The regression (in a chronological sense only) to a classical perspective with its removal of the expectation of growth and industrialisation may prove to offer not only a more realistic and persuasive context for understanding of the Chinese experience but valuable insights into the European experience [15].

Contact with the West was both beneficial and damaging and, like the interaction between the modern and traditional sectors, involved both stimulus and restraint. The West was instrumental in creating the modern industrial sector and in furthering its development, and it contributed to the intensification of commercialisation which was taking place within the agricultural sector. Some Chinese producers in the modern sector were 'oppressed' and some farmers succumbed to the additional risks that dependence on the market brought, but the majority benefited. Handicraft producers found their position undermined by the availability of machine-made goods but also came to rely on the products of the modern sector for their survival. In the face of these pressures and opportunities Chinese industry proved to be highly adaptive and innovatory.

Within agriculture there was a wide diversity of experience in response to population pressure and widening market opportunities. The majority of households continued to live in poverty and defended themselves against diminishing farm size by embracing cash cropping and allocating more labour resources to handicraft pursuits. Survival through traditional subsistence crops became increasingly untenable. Without recourse to commercialisation and the familisation of production survival was no longer possible, though the experience of the 1930s confirmed that even heightened commercialism could not guarantee it. Many peasants were forced to increase labour inputs more rapidly than output could be raised and the marginal productivity of their labour declined. For others, and largely those with above average access to land, commercialisation could facilitate higher productivity and upward mobility.

The role of the state also changed significantly. At the outset its function was to maintain the status quo. The decline in its military and political authority – sometimes gradual, sometimes rapid, sometimes temporarily reversed – paralleled an increasing intervention in economic and societal processes. Modern industry was too important to be left to private enterprise and needed to be controlled. By the late 1930s a substantial proportion had fallen into 'bureaucratic' hands. In agriculture the state was increasingly forced to balance between interventions designed to protect the people's livelihood and the maintenance of support from the landlord–gentry elite. It antagonised both peasants and landlords and did nothing to raise the level of investment. In general policy remained internal rather than external in its focus, and the state never controlled a sufficient proportion of the nation's resources to change decisively the course of economic development.

The major long-term influences on the process and extent of economic change were the pressure of population on the land, the intensification of commercialised market mechanisms, contact with the outside world and the role of the state. By the middle of the twentieth century those factors had combined and inter-related to produce an economy which contained significant elements of modernisation but not an economy which can be confirmed with certainty as having achieved the onset of sustained growth. It was also, in the short term, an economy suffering the effects of more than a decade of war and economic mismanagement. These legacies, together with the particular learning process which the leaders of the new Communist government had undergone, were to have a significant influence on subsequent economic development.

The policy response evolved by the Communist leadership was not just the product of its Marxist ideology; it was also influenced by the socio-economic and ecological conditions encountered in the limited areas of rural control which the military realities of the time dictated. Jiang Jieshi's coup of April 1927 forced the CCP to re-orientate as a rural rather than an urban revolutionary party. Minor, but still significant, Party figures such as Mao Zedong and Peng Pai (P'eng P'ai) had already come to recognise the revolutionary potential of the peasantry and it was Mao who was to remain at the centre of the evolution of revolutionary policies for rural development [78].

The basic CCP position was a 'distributionist' one. The root of the rural problem was seen as exploitation stemming from the unequal distribution of land ownership in favour of the landlord class. Ten per cent of the population (landlords and rich peasants) were deemed to own 70–80 per cent of the land, ensuring poverty for the majority and preventing development in the rural economy [73]. The solution was the redistribution of land from rich to poor. The high degree of inequality would enable all households to be made self sufficient and brought up to self-sufficient middle-peasant status. The material welfare of the poor would be improved and the resources for increased output released.

In fact the premise for this 'absolute egalitarianism' turned out to be a false one. In most areas there simply was not enough confiscated land available to enable equality to be reached at subsistence level [63; 84]. Moreover, as the strategic needs of China's future industrialisation began to loom larger in the late 1940s, the prospect of destroying the productive capacity of the most efficient farmers (rich peasants) determined that the scale of confiscation was curtailed at the inevitable expense of the poor. The position of the poor was significantly improved (they received land and rent payments were abolished) and landlord economic power was destroyed. But middle peasants were also allocated land and the position of rich peasants was protected (only land rented out to others was confiscated) [88]. Productive relations in the countryside were more egalitarian but equality was not absolute [83]. It was a recognition that the majority could not be brought up to subsistence level from their farming activities alone.

Superficially, the Communist revolution had succeeded in creating capitalism rather than socialism in the countryside. Peasants owned their own land, they were encouraged to produce for revived rural markets and they were exhorted to become rich. Yet within this new system elements of socialism were already apparent. Mao's concept of 'New Democracy' involved the creation of the seeds of socialism within capitalism rather than the creation of capitalism as an end in itself [54: vol. II, 344]. Mutual aid, the first step towards collectivisation, was already an integral part of the land revolution by 1950 [84].

Other features of subsequent Maoist strategy were also evident. In Yan'an (Yenan) – the CCP stronghold after the Long March – ideas on small-scale rural industrialisation, self-sufficiency, decentralised decision making, moral incentives, emulation campaigns and *xia xiang* ('down to the countryside') movements took hold. The development of rural industry both within the household and, on a larger scale, in co-operative ventures was given particular prominence [57; 58; 88; 151]. Whilst there must be a question-mark over whether policies evolved in a poor, backward and isolated area during a period of extreme military pressure could be relevant at the national level in a post-war context, all were to feature prominently in both the Great Leap Forward (1958–60) and the Cultural Revolution (1966–76).

In 1949 the new Communist government faced an economy devastated by war and hyper-inflation [56]. It was inexperienced in urban industrialisation and highly distrustful of the existing Treaty Port society [127]. Yet a number of factors combined to facilitate the rehabilitation of the economy. To begin with a substantial modern sector already existed. It was more a question of bringing capacity back into production than of creating it [102]. Secondly, the concentration of assets in bureaucratic hands under the Nationalists made it possible to acquire direct and immediate control over most of the heavy and strategic industries. The same was true for the Japanese assets in Manchuria, although here the situation was complicated by the removal of plant and machinery by the Soviet forces as they withdrew. In addition, the new government was able to requisition a sizeable agrarian surplus in order to finance industrialisation. Even if Riskin's estimate that agricultural output exceeded basic subsistence requirements by the equivalent of almost 20 per cent of GNP in 1933 is an over-statement, it was possible for the government to tax a substantial proportion of rural output and still allow average welfare in the countryside to rise [77; 93]. Finally, the government had earned the military and moral authority to rule and was well on the way to creating the administrative structure extending down to grass-roots level necessary to exercise that authority effectively. This, together with effects of the Second World War on the Western powers in China, also enabled the government to initiate measures to exclude the West from China if it wished.

By the end of 1952 the government had achieved a remarkable economic rehabilitation. Land reform was virtually complete, inflation had been brought under control, output was back to peak pre-war levels and a new institutional framework had been put into place. However, the underlying problem of how to achieve development in a labour-abundant–land-scarce agricultural economy remained. The government faced two choices. One was to continue with its initial market-based, material incentive approach, through which the development of a rich peasant-led agricultural economy might overcome the 'involutionary' or Smithian growth of the past and create the resources for balanced socialist industrialisation. The other was to embrace Soviet command-planning strategy in order to press forward immediately into and through socialism. In economic terms, if no other, the adoption of the latter proved a misguided and costly mistake though it might, ironically and belatedly, have provided the base from which late twentieth-century 'capitalism with Chinese characteristics' could develop successfully in the post-Mao era. The transformation of the rural economy since the late 1970s, in particular, bears more than a passing resemblance to the proto-industrialisation of the past.

Bibliography

A. General historical overviews

[1]   Chao Kang (1986) *Man and Land in Chinese History: An Economic Analysis* (Stanford)

[2]   Cohen, P. (1984) *Discovering History in China: American Historical Writing on the Recent Chinese Past* (New York)

[3]   Eastman, L. (1988) *Family, Field, and Ancestors: Constancy and Change in China's Social and Economic History 1550–1949* (New York)

[4]   Elvin, M. (1973) *The Pattern of the Chinese Past: A Social and Economic Interpretation* (Stanford)

[5]   Elvin, M. (1984) 'Why China failed to create an endogenous industrial capitalism: a critique of Max Weber's explanation', *Theory and Society* 13

[6]   Elvin, M. (1989) 'Making progress pay – a basic problem in China's early economic modernisation', in *Second Conference on Modern Chinese Economic History* (Taipei)

[7]   Faure, D. (1994) *China and Capitalism: Business Enterprise in Modern China* (Hong Kong)

[8]   Hamilton, G. (1985) 'Why no capitalism in China? Negative questions in historical comparative research', in A. Buss (ed.), *Max Weber in Asian Studies* (Leiden)

[9]   Huang, P. (1991) 'The paradigmatic crisis in Chinese studies: paradoxes in social and economic history', *Modern China* 17.3

[10]   Little, D. (1989) *Understanding Peasant China: Case Studies in the Philosophy of Social Science* (New Haven)

[11]   Moulder, Frances (1977) *Japan, China, and the Modern World Economy: Toward a Reinterpretation of East Asian Development, ca. 1600 to ca. 1918* (Cambridge)

[12]   Myers, R. (1978) *The Chinese Economy: Past and Present* (Belmont, Calif.)

[13]   Spence, J. (1982) *The Gate of Heavenly Peace: The Chinese and Their Revolution* (London)
[14]   Spence, J. (1991) *The Search for Modern China* (New York)
[15]   Wong, R. Bin (1997) *China Transformed: Historical Change and the Limits of European Experience* (Ithaca, N.Y.)
[16]   Wrigley, E. (1988) *Continuity, Chance and Change: The Character of the Industrial Revolution in England* (Cambridge)

B. Edited collections of papers

[17]   Brown, I. (ed.) (1989) *The Economies of Asia and Africa in the Inter-war Depression* (London)
[18]   Brown, R. (ed.) (1996) *Chinese Business Enterprise* (London)
[19]   Fairbank, J. (ed.) (1978) *The Cambridge History of China*, vol. x: *Late Ch'ing, 1800–1911, Part 1* (Cambridge)
[20]   Fairbank, J. and Liu Kwang-ching (eds.) (1980) *The Cambridge History of China*, vol. xi: *Late Ch'ing, 1800–1911, Part 2* (Cambridge)
[21]   Fairbank, J.(ed.) (1983) *The Cambridge History of China*, vol. xii: *Republican China, 1912–49, Part 1* (Cambridge)
[22]   Fairbank, J. and Feuerwerker, A (eds.) (1986) *The Cambridge History of China*, vol. xiii: *Republican China, 1912–49, Part 2* (Cambridge)
[23]   Hou Chi-ming and Yu Tzong-shian (eds.) (1979) *Modern Chinese Economic History. Proceedings of the Conference on Modern Chinese Economic History* (Taipei)
[24]   Huang, P. (ed.) (1978) *The Development of Underdevelopment* (New York)
[25]   Leonard, Jane and Watt, J. (eds.) (1992) *To Achieve Security and Wealth: The Qing Imperial State and the Economy, 1644–1911* (Ithaca, N.Y.)
[26]   Lieberthal, K., Kallgren, J., MacFarquhar, R. *et al.* (1991) *Perspectives on Modern China: Four Anniversaries* (Armonk, N.Y.)
[27]   Perkins, D. (ed.) (1975) *China's Modern Economy in Historical Perspective* (Stanford)
[28]   Pong, D. and Fung, S. (eds.) (1985) *Ideal and Reality: Social and Political Change in Modern China, 1860–1949* (Lanham)
[29]   Rawski, T. and Li, Lillian (eds.) (1992) *Chinese History in Economic Perspective* (Berkeley)
[30]   Skinner, G. (ed.) (1977) *The City in Late Imperial China* (Stanford)
[31]   Willmott, E. (ed.) (1972) *Economic Organisation in Chinese Society* (Stanford)
[32]   Wright, T. (ed.) (1992) *The Chinese Economy in the Early Twentieth Century: Recent Chinese Studies* (London)

C. The early to mid Qing economy

[33] Fairbank, J. (1978) 'Introduction: the old order', in [19]

[34] Fairbank, J. (1978) 'The creation of the treaty system', in [19]

[35] Hamilton, G. and Lai Chi-kong (1989) 'Consumerism without capitalism: consumption and brand names in late Imperial China', in H. Rutz and B. Orlove (eds.), *The Social Economy of Consumption* (Lanham)

[36] Lai Chi-kong (1995) 'The historiography of maritime China since *c.* 1975', *Research in Maritime History* 9

[37] Mann Jones, S. and Kuhn, P. (1978) 'Dynastic decline and the roots of rebellion', in [19]

[38] Naquin, S. and Rawski, E. (1987) *Chinese Society in the Eighteenth Century* (New Haven)

[39] Wakeman, F., Jnr (1978) 'The Canton trade and the Opium War', in [19]

[40] Zelin, Madeleine (1991) 'The structure of the Chinese economy during the Qing period: some thoughts on the 150th anniversary of the Opium War', in [26]

D. The late Qing economy (*c.* 1850–1911)

[41] Chang Chung-li (1962) *The Income of the Chinese Gentry* (Seattle)

[42] Feuerwerker, A. (1958) *China's Early Industrialisation: Sheng Hsuan-huai (1844–1916) and Mandarin Enterprise* (Cambridge, Mass.)

[43] Feuerwerker, A. (1969) *The Chinese Economy, ca. 1870–1911* (Ann Arbor)

[44] Hao Yen-p'ing (1986) *The Commercial Revolution in Nineteenth-Century China: The Rise of Sino-Western Mercantile Capitalism* (Berkeley)

[45] King, F. (1965) *Money and Monetary Policy in China 1845–1895* (Cambridge, Mass.)

[46] Kuhn, P. (1978) 'The Taiping Rebellion', in [20]

[47] Liu Kwang-ching (1980) 'The Ch'ing Restoration', in [20]

[48] Liu Ts'ui-jung (1985) *Trade on the Han River and its Impact on Economic Development, c. 1800–1911* (Taipei)

[49] McElderry, Andrea (1996) 'Securing trust and stability; Chinese finance in the late nineteenth century', in [18]

E. The Republican economy 1911–1949

[50] Bergère, Marie-Claire (1983) 'The Chinese bourgeoisie, 1911–37', in [21]

[51]   Eastman, L. (1974) *The Abortive Revolution: China under Nationalist Rule, 1927–1937* (Cambridge, Mass.)

[52]   Eastman, L. (1984) *Seeds of Destruction: Nationalist China in War and Revolution, 1937–49* (Stanford)

[53]   Feuerwerker, A. (1977) *Economic Trends in the Republic of China, 1912–1949* (Ann Arbor)

[54]   Mao Zedong (1954–61) *The Selected Works of Mao Tse-tung*, vols. I–IV (Beijing)

[55]   Myers, R. (1989) 'The world depression and the Chinese economy 1930–6', in [17]

[56]   Pepper, Suzanne (1989) *Civil War in China: The Political Struggle* (Berkeley)

[57]   Schran, P. (1976) *Guerilla Economy: The Development of the Shensi-Kansu-Ninghsia Border Region, 1937–1945* (Albany)

[58]   Selden, M. (1971) *The Yenan Way in Revolutionary China* (Cambridge, Mass.)

[59]   Sheridan, J. (1975) *China in Disintegration: The Republican Era in Chinese History, 1912–1949* (New York)

[60]   Sih, P. (ed.) (1977) *Nationalist China During the Sino-Japanese War, 1937–45* (Hicksville, N.Y.)

[61]   Wang Yuru (1992) 'Economic development in China between the two world wars (1920–1936)', in [32]

F. Agriculture

[62]   Ash, R. (1976) *Land Tenure in Pre-Revolutionary China; Kiangsu Province in the 1920s and 1930s* (London)

[63]   Ash, R. (1976) 'Economic aspects of land reform in Kiangsu', Parts I and II, *China Quarterly*

[64]   Bell, Linda (1992) 'Farming, sericulture, and peasant rationality in Wuxi county in the early twentieth century', in [29]

[65]   Bernhardt, Kathryn (1992) *Rents, Taxes and Peasant Resistance: The Lower Yangzi Region, 1840–1950* (Stanford)

[66]   Brandt, L. (1985) 'Chinese Agriculture and the International Economy, 1870s–1930s: A Reassessment', *Explorations in Economic History* 22

[67]   Brandt, L. (1989) *Commercialization and Agricultural Development: Central and Eastern China 1870–1937* (Cambridge)

[68]   Buck, J. (1964) *Land Utilization in China* (New York)

[69]   Buck, J., Dawson, O. and Wu Yuan-li (1966) *Food and Agriculture in Communist China* (London)

[70]   Crooks, D. and I. (1979) *Mass Movement in a Chinese Village: Ten Mile Inn* (London)

[71] Ding Changqing (1992) 'The development of capitalism in modern Chinese agriculture', in [32]

[72] Esherick, J. (1981) 'Number Games: a note on land distribution in pre revolutionary China', *Modern China* 7.4

[73] Faure, D. (1989) *The Rural Economy of Pre-Liberation China* (Hong Kong)

[74] Fei Hsiao-tung and Chang Chih-i (1949) *Earthbound China, A Study of Rural Economy in Yunnan* (London)

[75] Huang, P. (1985) *The Peasant Economy and Social Change in North China* (Stanford)

[76] Huang, P. (1990) *The Peasant Family and Rural Development in the Yangzi Delta, 1350–1988* (Stanford)

[77] Lippit, V. (1974) *Land Reform and Economic Development in China: A Study of Institutional Change and Development Finance* (White Plains, N.Y.)

[78] Marks, R. (1984) *Rural Revolution in South China: Peasants and the Making of History in Haifeng County* (Madison)

[79] Myers, R. (1970) *The Chinese Peasant Economy: Agricultural Development in Hopei and Shandong, 1890–1949* (Cambridge, Mass.)

[80] Myers, R. (1978) 'Wheat in China – past, present and future', *China Quarterly* 27

[81] Myers, R. (1986) 'The Agrarian System', in [22]

[82] Perkins, D. (1969) *Agricultural Development in China 1368–1968* (Edinburgh)

[83] Roll, C. (1980) *The Distribution of Rural Incomes in China* (New York)

[84] Shue, Vivienne (1980) *Peasant China in Transition: The Dynamics of Development towards Socialism, 1949–1956* (Berkeley)

[85] Skinner, G. W. (1964–5) 'Marketing and social structure in rural China, Parts 1–111', *Journal of Asian Studies* 24.1–3

[86] Tawney, R. H. (1932) *Land and Labour in China* (London)

[87] Thompson, R. (trans.) (1990) *Mao Zedong: Report from Xunwu* (Stanford)

[88] Wong, J. (1973) *Land Reform in the People's Republic of China* (New York)

G. Growth and structural change

[89] Brandt, L. (1997) 'Reflections on China's late 19th and early 20th-century economy', *China Quarterly* 150

[90] Liu Ta-chung and Yeh Kung-chia (1965) *The Economy of the Chinese Mainland: National Income and Economic Development* (Princeton)

[91] Perkins, D. (1975) 'Growth and structural change of China's twentieth century economy', in [27]

[92] Rawski, T. (1989) *Economic Growth in Pre-war China* (Berkeley)

[93] Riskin, C. (1975) 'Surplus and stagnation in modern China', in [27]

[94] Yeh Kung-chia (1979) 'China's national income, 1931–1936', in [23]

H. Modern industry

[95] Brown, R. (1996) 'Chinese business in an institutional and historical perspective', in [18]

[96] Chang, J. (1969) *Industrial Development in Pre-Communist China: A Quantitative Analysis* (Edinburgh)

[97] Chao Kang (1977) *The Development of Cotton Textile Production in China* (Cambridge, Mass.)

[98] Faure, D. (1996) 'The control of equity in Chinese firms within the modern sector from the late Qing to the early Republic', in [18]

[99] Gardella, R. (1992) 'Squaring accounts: commercial bookkeeping methods and capitalist rationalism in late Qing and Republican China', *Journal of Asian Studies* 51.2

[100] Kirby, W. (1995) 'China incorporated: company law and business enterprise in twentieth century China', *Journal of Asian Studies* 54.1

[101] Kraus, R. (1968) 'Cotton and cotton goods in China, 1918–1936', Ph.D. Dissertation, Harvard University

[102] Rawski, T. (1980) *China's Transition to Industrialism: Producer Goods and Economic Development in the Twentieth Century* (Ann Arbor)

[103] Wright, T. (1984) *Coal Mining in China's Economy and Society 1895–1937* (Cambridge)

[104] Zhang Zhongli (1992) 'The development of Chinese national capital in the 1920s', in [32]

I. Handicrafts

[105] Chao Kang (1975) 'The growth of a modern cotton textile industry and competition with handicrafts', in [27]

[106] Elvin, M. (1972) 'The high-level equilibrium trap: the causes of the decline of invention in the traditional Chinese textile industries', in [31]

[107] Feuerwerker, A. (1970) 'Handicraft and manufactured cotton textiles in China, 1871–1910', *Journal of Economic History* 30

[108] Li, Lillian (1981) *China's Silk Trade: Traditional Industry in the Modern World, 1842–1937* (Cambridge, Mass.)

[109] Mann, Susan (1992) 'Household handicrafts and state policy in Qing times', in [25]

[110] Myers, R. (1965) 'Cotton textile handicrafts and the development of the cotton textile industry in modern China', *Economic History Review* 18.3

[111] Xu Xinwu (1988) 'The struggle of the handicraft cotton industry against machine textiles in China', *Modern China* 14.1

[112] Xu Xinwu (1992) 'The process of the disintegration of modern China's natural economy', in [32]

J. Foreign trade and investment

[113] Bergère, Marie-Claire (1989) 'The consequences of the post First World War depression for the China treaty-port economy 1921–3', in [17]

[114] Chen Nai-ruenn (1979) 'China's balance of payments:the experience of financing a long-term trade deficit in the twentieth century', in [23]

[115] Cheng Yu-kwei (1978) *Foreign Trade and Industrial Development of China* (Westpoint, Conn.)

[116] Cochran, S. (1980) *Big Business in China: Sino-Foreign Rivalry in the Cigarette Industry,1890–1930* (Cambridge, Mass.)

[117] Dernberger, R. (1975) 'The role of the foreigner in China's economic development', in [27]

[118] Ding Richu and Shen Zuwei (1992) 'Foreign trade and China's economic modernisation', in [32]

[119] Greenburg, M. (1951) *British Trade and the Opening of China, 1800–42* (Cambridge)

[120] Hou Chi-ming (1965) *Foreign Investment and Economic Development in China 1840–1937* (Cambridge, Mass.)

[121] Hsiao Liang-lin (1974) *China's Foreign Trade Statistics' 1864–1949* (Cambridge, Mass.)

[122] Johnson, Linda Cooke (1995) *Shanghai from Market Town to Treaty Port, 1074–1858* (Stanford)

[123] Liu Foding (1992) 'Foreign capital and China's traditional economy', in [32]

[124] MacGregor, D. (1961) *The China Bird* (London)

[125] Mah Feng-hwa (1979) 'External influence and Chinese economic development: a re-examination', in [23]

[126] Marriner, S. (1961) *Rathbones of Liverpool, 1845–73* (Liverpool)

[127] Murphey, R. (1970) *The Treaty Ports and China's Modernisation: What Went Wrong?* (Ann Arbor)

[128] Murphey, R. (1977) *The Outsiders: The Western Experience in India and China* (Ann Arbor)

[129] Remer, C. (1933) *Foreign Investment in China* (New York)

K. State and the economy

[130] Chan, W. (1977) *Merchants, Mandarins and Modern Enterprise in Late Ch'ing China* (Cambridge, Mass.)

[131] Chan, W. (1980) 'Government, merchants and industry to 1911', in [20]

[132] Ch'en, J. (1980) *State Economic Policies of the Ch'ing Government 1840–1895* (New York)

[133] Chu, S. and Liu Kwang-ching (eds.) (1994) *Li Hung-chang and China's Early Modernisation* (Armonk, N.Y.)

[134] Coble, P. (1977) *The Shanghai Capitalist Class and the Nationalist Government, 1927–37* (Stanford)

[135] Gangulee, N. (ed.) (1945) *The Teachings of Sun Yat-sen: Selections from his Writings* (London)

[136] Hou Chi-ming (1977) 'Economic development and public finance in China, 1937–1945', in [60]

[137] Kindermann, G.-K. (ed.) (1982) *Sun Yat-sen: Founder and Symbol of China's Revolutionary Nation-building* (Munich)

[138] Kirby, W. (1984) *Germany and Republican China* (Stanford)

[139] Kuo Ting-yee and Liu Kwang-ching (1978) 'Self-strengthening: the pursuit of Western technology', in [20]

[140] Lai Chi-kong (1992) 'The Qing state and merchant enterprise: the China Merchants' Company, 1872–1902', in [25]

[141] Leonard, Jane (1992) 'The state's resources and the people's livelihood (guoji minsheng): the Daoguang Emperor's dilemmas about Grand Canal restoration, 1825', in [25]

[142] Nolan, P. (1993) *State and Market in the Chinese Economy: Essays on Controversial Issues* (London)

[143] Perdue, P. (1987) *Exhausting the Earth: State and Peasant in Hunan, 1500–1850* (Cambridge, Mass.)

[144] Perkins, D. (1967) 'Government as an obstacle to industrialization: the case of nineteenth century China', *Journal of Economic History* 27.4

[145] Pomeranz, K. (1993) *The Making of a Hinterland: State, Society and Economy in Inland North China, 1853–1937* (Berkeley)

[146] Pong, D. (1993) *Shen Pao-chen and China's Modernization in the Nineteenth Century* (Cambridge)

[147] Reardon-Anderson, J. (1991) *The Study of Change: Chemistry in China, 1840–1949* (Cambridge)

[148] Sun E-tu Zen (1992) 'The finance ministry (hubu) and its relationship to the private economy in Qing times', in [25]

[149] Sun Yat-sen (n.d.) *San Min Chu I: The Three Principles of the People* (Taipei)

[150] Wakeman, F. (1991) 'Models of historical change: the Chinese state and society, 1839–1989', in [26]

[151] Watson, A. (ed.) (1980) *Mao Zedong and the Political Economy of the Border Region: A Translation of Mao's Economic and Financial Problems* (Cambridge)

[152] Will, P.-E. and Wong, R. Bin (1991) *Nourish the People: The State Civilian Granary System in China, 1650–1850* (Ann Arbor)

[153] Wright, Mary Clabaugh (1957) *The Last Stand of Chinese Conservatism: The T'ung-chih Restoration, 1862–1874* (Stanford)

[154] Wright, T. (1985) 'The Nationalist state and regulation of Chinese industry during the Nanjing decade: competition and control in coal mining', in [28]

[155] Wright, T. (1991) 'Coping with the world depression: the Nationalist government's relations with Chinese industry and commerce, 1932–36', *Modern Asian Studies* 25.4

[156] Young, A. (1971) *China's Nation-Building Effort, 1927–37* (Stanford)

L. The Huang–Rawski debate

[157] Brandt, L. (1987) 'Review of Huang 1985', *Economic Development and Cultural Change* 35.3

[158] Feuerwerker, A. (1990) 'An old question revisited: was the glass half-full or half-empty for China's agriculture before 1949?, *Peasant Studies* 17.3

[159] Gottchang, T. (1992) 'Incomes in the Chinese rural economy, 1885–1935:comments on the debate', *Republican China* 18.1

[160] Hartford, K. (1992) 'Will the real Chinese peasant please stand up?', *Republican China* 18.1

[161] Huang, P. (1992) 'The study of rural China's economic history', *Republican China* 18.1

[162] Huang, P. (1991) 'A reply to Ramon Myers', *Journal of Asian Studies* 50.3

[163] Little, D. (1992) 'New perspectives on the Chinese rural economy, 1885–1935', *Republican China* 18.1

[164] Myers, R. (1991) 'How did the modern Chinese economy develop? – A review article', *Journal of Asian Studies* 50.3

[165] Rawski, T. (1992) 'Ideas about studying China's rural economy: a comment on the commentaries', *Republican China* 18.1

[166] Wiens, T. (1992) 'Trends in the late Qing and Republican rural economy: reality or myth?', *Republican China* 18.1

[167] Wong, R. Bin (1990) 'The development of China's peasant economy: a new formulation of an old problem', *Peasant Studies* 17.3

[168] Wong, R. Bin (1992) 'Chinese economic history and development: a note on the Myers–Huang exchange', *Journal of Asian Studies* 51.3

M. Demographic change

[169] Ho Ping-ti (1959) *Studies in the Population of China* (Cambridge, Mass.)

[170] Lee, J. and Campbell, C. (1997) *Fate and Fortune in Rural China: Social Organisation and Population Behavior in Liaoning 1774–1873* (Cambridge)

[171] Schran, P. (1978) 'China's demographic evolution 1850–1953 reconsidered', *China Quarterly* 75

N. Price trends

[172] Li, Lillian (1992) 'Grain prices in Zhili Province, 1736–1911', in [29]

[173] Wang Yeh-chien (1992) 'Secular trends of rice prices in the Yangzi delta, 1638–1935', in [29]

[174] Bessler, D. (1990) 'A note on Chinese rice prices: interior markets, 1928–1931', *Explorations in Economic History* 27

O. Manchuria

[175] Bix, H. (1972) 'Japanese imperialism and the Manchurian economy', *China Quarterly* 51

[176] Chao Kang (1982) *The Economic Development of Manchuria: The Rise of a Frontier Economy* (Ann Arbor)

[177] Duus, P., Myers, R. and Peattie, M. (1989) *The Japanese Informal Empire in China, 1895–1937* (Princeton)

[178] Jones, F. (1949) *Manchuria since 1931* (London)

Index

New Studies in Economic and Social History

Titles in the series available from Cambridge University Press

Previously published as
Studies in Economic and Social History

Titles in the series available from the Macmillan Press Limited

Economic History Society

The Economic History Society, which numbers around 3,000 members, publishes the *Economic History Review* four times a year (free to members) and holds an annual conference.

Enquiries about membership should be addressed to

The Assistant Secretary
Economic History Society
PO Box 70
Kingswood
Bristol
BS15 5TB

Full-time students may join at special rates.